The Art of
Peaceful and Happy Living

Dr. (Mrs.) Shantha N Nair

Originals
Delhi-110052

First Published 2016

ISBN 10: 81-8454-159-7
ISBN 13: 978-81-8454-159-5

Published By
Originals
A-6, Second Floor, Nimri Commercial Centre,
Ashok Vihar Phase-4, Delhi - 110 052 (India)
Tel.: +91 11 2730 2453 Fax: 011 4706 1936
website: www.Lppindia.com
e-mail: info@Lppindia.com

Printed At
D K Fine Art Press P Ltd.
Delhi-110052

PRINTED IN INDIA

Dedicated to my husband

Sri. K C N NAIR

Contents

Preface

The late twilight musings of the one who is passing through the late twilight period of her life is what this book is all about. When I look back and peep in to my past the various happenings of my life pass through my mind like the scenes in a movie- some happy, some sad, some fulfilling and some when I cursed myself, and so on. At this point of my life I feel like the one who is standing ready in the Railway plat form of life with all my luggage-the accumulated tendencies or thoughts or *Samskaras* to board the train, my carrier, that will arrive shortly for my unknown onward journey. I do not remember how many times I have stood like this in the Railway platforms safeguarding all my belongings, every time ready to board the train that was likely to arrive shortly.

For all my previous journeys till today in my present life, I had to reserve my ticket to a specific place well in advance, to travel on a specific date by a specific train and when the train arrived on the platform, get into the train, sit in my allotted seat after boarding the train and pass through several stations and places to reach the destination that I know well in advance. Contrary to this, in the final journey of one's life one does not know when the train will arrive at the station, the stations and places he has to pass through during his journey and also the time the journey would take to reach the destination that is unknown. This journey also needed no advance booking as the tickets were already booked for our return journey by our creator Himself when He sent us to this world. So life is a journey to some known destinations or finally to an unknown destination. We have come to this world only to go and perhaps to come again only to go back again. The only difference is that while some leave the world early, some others leave after some time. When that is so why can't we make our limited, present (of this birth) stay in this world the most happy, peaceful, and make our life on earth as human beings purposeful and worthy? After all is it not the very goal and purpose of our life, of our very existence on earth as human beings?

While these thoughts were passing through my mind, all the memories both happy and sad, good and bad of my life came up in my mind and I asked myself these questions. Did I make my life so far the best one or at least the best possible one? If not, then, why not? Is it not possible for all human beings to make their life at least the best possible, so that they make their life worthy and purposeful and be happy and peaceful till they breathe their last and make all others around them enjoy the same happiness and peace? Can't they by their thoughts, words and deeds make themselves and those around them feel happy and peaceful, that is the very goal of human life? How did I behave in my life? Did I try to maximize my efforts to fill myself with positive thoughts, words and acts that made my life and that of the others happy and peaceful? Now I understand all the negative emotions in me like anger, hatred, jealousy, pride, enmity etc. did not make me or the others happy at all either immediately or after sometime, then or now. On the contrary did not my good emotions that I consider as positive bring back immense joy and peace of mind ultimately to me as well as for those around me? Did I really and honestly try to make my life happy, peaceful, worthy and purposeful for myself and for the others? What is my honest answer for all these questions? These and other such similar questions made me admit the fact that I did not do my best to make my life the best or at least the best possible one and this thought made me feel that I did not do justice to my life so far. Not that I was a very bad person who was full of all negativity. At least I do not think so. But when I introspect I realize that I had a significant or considerable share of negativity in me that made me and the others around me fill with negative emotions that depleted the physical and mental energy of both myself and that of the others as my negativity affected not only the others on whom they were targeted at but it also had a negative impact on me and the strangest part of it was that even though my negativity was intended for or even targeted at some other person it was I who was affected immediately and more negatively by that and that made me realize that my negative emotions and thoughts had their harmful effects more upon me, on my physical and mental wellbeing and health than that of the others on whom they were aimed at.

Now, at this stage of my life I very clearly understand that it was my ignorance and lack of knowledge and understanding that made me fail to recognize, understand and feel grateful for all the unbounded love, affection, selflessness and sacrifice of my parents as I took for granted all that they did for me. After the demise of my mother my father was staying with us during his last days and now when I recollect I will have to admit that I failed to spend enough time to be with him, sit by his side and talk to him on matters that could have made him forget his physical pain and discomfort and mental depression and could have made him happier.

Such an act that I could have done frequently by talking about him, our childhood days with our parents, his days when he was in service as the Assistant Director of surveys and Land records of the composite, the then Madras state and a little mention in a very subtle manner of the sacrifices made by our parents for making our life happy and comfortable and so on would have made him relive the cherished moments of his earlier days and would have rejuvenated him and empowered him beyond any limit that I could visualize. My ill health coupled with my mental condition of depression after I lost my second son as a still born baby at that time might have been the reasons for my lack of adequate understanding of my father who was then bed ridden for a couple of months due to a fracture of his hip bone. But all my justifications for my lack of understanding of my father's psychology during his last days when he became bedridden, I consider now as mere escapism on my part. The fact is I did fail in that particular aspect. Again it was my possessiveness and expectations from my husband and my son after he grew up, the expectations from my brother and my sisters and my sense of ego in the case of others that generated all the negativities in me. Is this for what man lives in this world? At this stage I find that only those who are not possessive, are humble and with least expectations from anything or any person gain in life. They are bound to be happy and peaceful till their end. They also gain respect and love from all others; whereas the other category of people who are possessive, full of ego and expectations not only do not gain anything in life but also lose all love, respect and affection in this world. They not only do not gain but also lose happiness and peace in their life. That is the truth of life.

Every one without any exception knows honestly that he can become happy and peaceful only when he has positive thoughts that lead to happiness and peace not only for himself but also for all the others around him. All positive emotions just as the negative ones will have their effects more on the sender than on the recipient and now at this period of my life when I recollect my past experiences of life I realize that while I benefited more from my own positivity that sent positive vibrations to the others I also suffered more adversely and intensely than the other person when I projected and radiated my negative emotions or feelings that caused negative vibrations all around me causing pain and hardship both to myself as well as for the others around me. So it is clear to me now that only the positive feelings and thoughts that give rise to positive words and actions will make every one of us happy and peaceful and make one's life purposeful and worthy and this is what every human being without any exception craves for. When that is the case is it not a fact that I spent most of my life with many negative emotions that prevented me from achieving the very goal of my life? Is it enough if I merely acknowledge my negativity, repent and continue to think and feel bad about all my negative emotions? Shouldn't my negative behavior make me learn from my experience and bring about a change for better in me as mere brooding over the past is of no use because nothing can alter that, that is already over? Is there a way out? If there is, then what is that way? Can I rectify my mistakes of the past? If so how? Is it not too late for me now because I am already over seventy years old? But then why can't I make a small beginning at least now? Why can't I improve myself at least now so that I will not have any feeling of guilt and repentance for not thinking, speaking and doing the right thing at least now? Such thoughts led me to contemplate on myself so that I can, with my limited possibility try to transform and benefit myself and also the others at least now as it is better late than never. This thought gave me some inspiration and I began to ponder over and analyze all that I had read in the course of my life so far particularly the ancient Indian scriptures, the discourses of spiritual masters and mystics that I listened to, the books that I read till now about spirituality, the websites that I could come across about this subject and more than everything my own experiences in my life and my observations of life around me and this book is the outcome of such thoughts and efforts. As Swami Vivekananda has said, we may read books, hear lectures, and talk miles but experience is the greatest teacher, the real eye opener. It is the best as it is, as we learn a lot while we live, through our own and that of the others' smiles and tears. So man learns as he lives. How far I am successful now in transforming my mind for the best possible results I do not know. But the one thing that I am certain is the fact that I have made a small beginning in this process and I feel some good is better than no good at all and so some beginning somewhere in one's life for one's own betterment is all that matters. I also believe that whatever sincere and honest efforts we make in our life for improving ourselves will have its own reward if not now at least later, if not in this birth but at least in some later birth. (I am a believer of Law of *Karma* and rebirth) What we sow we reap, what we give we get. Also, if our intentions are pure and honest then some unknown power or energy will be there to guide us whether we call it God, or the Supreme energy, or the Universal energy or the Creator who created all the creations of the world and the Universe itself, or some Divine energy, or the Cosmic law, or the very Absolute principle that is the ultimate, the greatest phenomenon.

After all our life is what we make it. We can either make it the best or the worst, happy or miserable.

The best possible life that is the result of a holistic health becomes possible only when all the three namely body, mind and spirit are healthy. While the physical health leads to mental or psychological health and vice versa one should know that it is the mental well- being that has greater power over the physical well-being than the reverse. Again the spiritual welfare no doubt depends upon both the physical as well as the mental well-being of a person. But even here it is the mental well-being rather than the physical health that plays an important role in uplifting one spiritually. That means mental well-being is the most important factor both for the physical as well as for the spiritual well-being of a man and this book is all about the mental well-being that brings about the physical health as well as spiritual elevation or enlightenment leading to everlasting happiness and peace for man.

I hope and wish that this book that is only a collection of my stray thoughts will serve as a guide for self-improvement for making life happy, peaceful, worthy and purposeful for those who are eager to improve themselves for achieving the best possible life by enhancing the positivity in them and by eliminating their negativity at least gradually so that they can enjoy a happy and peaceful life with the fulfillment during their final moments of life that after all they have not wasted their life as a human being, but instead they lived their life in a purposeful and worthy manner resulting in happiness and peace not only for themselves but also for those around them and this achievement in my opinion is no small achievement but undoubtedly the greatest of all achievements of any human being. When we were born we cried and our near and dear ones rejoiced. We should live our life in such a way that when we die and leave our physical body at least a few in this world if not all, cry and feel for us, while we as the mind , the subtle body, rejoice in our onward journey.

There are six chapters in this book. The entire subject matter of this book is in the form of questions and answers; the questions put by the author and the answers given by a *Sanyasi* who happens to be her co-traveller during her journey. The first chapter contains the twilight musings of the author while she is on a journey. It also tries to stress the importance of a vigilant mind that should not allow the negative tendencies to creep into it. A fictitious story is presented in this chapter to show how a man's life can be shattered by a split second evil or negative thought. The remaining five chapters deal with the subject matter of this book that includes Peace and Happiness through best possible life, negativity, positivity, the role of mind and the ways and means for achieving lasting peace and happiness in one's life.

1

The Prelude

The no. 1 platform of the *Tirupathi* Railway station was overflowing with people. *Tirupathi* being one of the most famous pilgrimage centers in the world, it attracted huge pilgrim population every day. As the announcement of the arrival of the train came all of us, my husband, myself, our son, our daughter in law, and our two little grand children who accompanied my husband and myself to the Railway station got ready and we walked to the spot where the B-2 compartment was supposed to halt. Soon the train arrived on the platform making a huge noise and slowly it stopped. Our compartment was a little away from the spot where we were standing. We somehow made our way through the thick crowd. Our son took our luggage and entered in to the compartment and we followed him. Our daughter in law and the kids stood near the door. After locating our allotted births our son kept the luggage underneath our seats and began to sermonize as usual. He began "Keep the phone on always so that I can contact you whenever I want. Shall I get you some magazines to read? Have your dinner as early as possible so that both of you can go to bed and get sufficient sleep. The train, if it is on time will reach *Palakkad* by 6.30 in the morning. Return to *Tirupathi* as soon as possible. Do not exert yourselves much. Take good rest. If you allow me I shall come to *Palakkad* to take you both back to *Tirupathi*. But always you both never allow me to accompany you".

Our son was going on. My husband interrupted him in the middle and said, "look, the train is about to start. Get down first. We are not as old and weak as you think us to be. When we really think that you should accompany us then we assure you that we will ask you for that. We heard all that you said. Take care." Then as our son was leaving we followed him up to the door and he got down from the train. Within a short time the train started moving and we stood near the door waving our hands until we could spot our children in that big crowd.

After returning to our seats my husband took out the water bottle and the bag that contained our dinner packets and placed it near my hand bag. As the schools and colleges have reopened after the summer vacation and also because many got down at the *Tirupathi* station there were vacant seats here and there. I sat near the window and began to relax as usual. I always enjoyed travelling, of course a comfortable one. The very idea of travelling to distant lands and far off places gave me a sense of thrill and happiness inside me. I always thought that more than books it is wide travelling that gave a lot of knowledge to one. But then one must also bear the discomforts and inconveniences that he may have to face when he steps out of his house where everything is as per his convenience and comfort. One must put up with the tiresomeness of the journey, the food, the accommodation and so on while travelling to different places and while staying in those places. Usually it is the time when I allowed my mind to wander enjoying and gazing at the sky and the beautiful scenery outside. Every place has its own beauty I thought- for that matter even a barren desert. The only thing is, you must have the necessary imagination to see the beauty that is contained there. It was late twilight and the Sun had almost set. The enchanting panoramic view of the sunset always fascinated me. The flocks of birds making a beautiful pattern on the sky were eagerly returning to their nests. Wherever the birds flew, far or near, they reached their nests before it was dark. Does it remind man about his final journey and destination? Perhaps yes-perhaps no- I do not know for certain. To me the sight seemed to convey the meaning that in the end all beings have to return to their original source from where they came. The retreating Sun and the darkness that gradually enveloped the whole atmosphere during twilight usually generated an inexplicable feeling inside me. At the same time such a sight also gave me a profound feeling of calmness inside that usually enabled me to concentrate on my late evening prayers in my small prayer room where I switched off the electric light after lighting the oil lamps. Invariably I liked only the dim, serene lights of the oil lamps when I prayed. It helped me to concentrate and calm down my wavering mind. Usually when I go to bed in the night I enjoyed gazing at the moonlit starry sky through the window until I fell asleep. At such times the vast, endless, silent sky always gave me a sense of connectivity with the mysterious Absolute consciousness, the supreme energy or power, our creator, and also with those near and dear ones who were dead and gone. Gradually darkness enveloped the whole atmosphere and nothing was visible from inside the compartment as it was totally dark outside with no moon light.

Suddenly my attention got diverted towards the two little children who were sitting opposite to me. They were fighting and screaming for the same toy that was lying in a corner uncared for and unwanted by both of them till then. The mother intervened as is usual everywhere, took the smaller one who was only nearly two years of age on her lap and began to divert the child's attention by showing something from the opposite direction while she gave the toy to the elder one who was nearly five years old. He happily took the toy with a triumphant look on his face and immersed himself in playing with it. How easy it is to divert the attention of little children, I thought. After playing with the toy for some time the elder one who got bored with it, left the toy there and began to nag the younger one. After all, this is how, we, the elders also behave. We do all possible things to fulfill our desires and very soon some other desires occupy our mind seeking fulfillment and this process goes on and on until the end of our life. When we are unable to fulfill our desires we become frustrated and negativity grips our mind with all its harmful consequences. The great souls are perfectly correct when they said that it is desire and the sense of ego that lead to attachment mainly towards people and objects and that is the root of all miseries, difficulties and unhappiness in life. While children fight for small toys we the elders fight for our possessions. That's all the difference.

After some time my thoughts turned towards our only son and precisely I recollected our conversation on that day during our lunch. In the course of our conversation our son asked me "*Amma*, what is the subject that you have chosen for your next book"? Smilingly I replied "I am yet to get a clear cut idea about that although I have some vague idea"

"What is it?" asked my son.

"I want to write something different this time".

"Different means? Most of your books so far were related to religion and spirituality and a few on Economics. Are you going to try some other field like your autobiography or something like that?"

"Oh, no, I am not such a great person to write my autobiography. There is nothing unique or great about my life I know."

"Then give me some clue about it as I am eager to know".

"I want to write something about the Art of Peaceful and Happy Living".

"Very good. It is an excellent idea. Unlike your earlier subjects that you have chosen for your books so far, this one, I think, will surely give you ample opportunity to be creative. Frankly speaking *Amma*, in all your books I liked your preface, the first chapter and the last chapters the most. No doubt all the middle chapters were quite informative. But readers want not merely information but more than that they also want to enjoy reading a book. Mere information however much you may try to present in an interesting manner will look like a text book. Look, there is no dearth of information in today's world. To me it looks that modern readers want information presented in a creative imaginative manner. Such books only are attracting more and more readers. This is my firm opinion. So now that you have chosen a subject that will offer you much opportunity for your imagination and creativity try to write the book in such a manner. See the result and then tell me."

"I know, I know. All that you have told me just now I totally agree. But it is not enough if one has got imagination inside oneself. He must also have the creative ability to express and present it in a very interesting manner. Every one for that matter is highly imaginative. For example the one who likes music very much and always enjoys listening to songs will be able to sing very well inside imaginatively although he may not be able to sing openly even a single line of the song properly. Anyone can carve out a figure from a stone like a sculptor mentally but it needs a lot of skill and inborn talent to become a sculptor. See, as you know I have been teaching Economics for nearly thirty nine years. Whenever I tried to make my point clear I invariably and unconsciously came out with facts and figures. So that means, I am not one who can express my ideas in a beautiful, poetic language. I know all the books that I wrote so far were not even text books but were only like guides that presented the subject matter in a very simple language and in a precise manner to benefit the average student, here, in this case, the common man. As you know I never thought that I will write so many books after my retirement. It is you who persuaded me to write books after I retired from service so that after a long period of hectic activity both at home and in the college I may not get bored. Even when you gave me the address of a publisher of books I was diffident to send the manuscript of what I wrote to him. When you compelled me, just to please you I agreed without the least expectation that the publisher would accept my work. But when my book was finally published it was such a moral boost to me and as you know that was the starting point of all my books that I wrote so far. That means I know my limitations".

"All that you have said just now I can understand because I know your nature thoroughly. You never venture unless you are persuaded continuously. Again, as far as I know many of the modern writers whose books have become quite popular all over the world are not professional writers. They are all from different fields or disciplines. Only when you attempt you will know whether you can or not. The difficulty with you is you always go on reading and listening to only spiritual and religious books and discourses. I have noticed from my childhood that you and *Acha* (father) had very little social life and social interaction even while you both were in service. You both think that social interaction means gossiping. But then, when we are social there are a lot of things that we can know and learn from other's lives for our own good as well as for that of the others. All right, at this stage you may want a quiet undisturbed life. I agree. But at least you can read fictions that are world famous. Whenever I bring any C D of a good movie and ask you to view it you say you are not interested. *Amma,* Don't' you think we can get a lot, a lot of knowledge from all these? Please try. You can and you will. Try to make your new book as creative as possible. Get some information from books and other sources that will help you in writing about this subject. But that must be only 25%. The remaining 75% should be your own imagination. You try to present the 25% information that you have collected in an interesting manner by connecting it with some incidents, stories, or dialogues or in any possible manner you like. I am sure your book will attract more readers than before".

"Look, I am a practical person not highly imaginative or creative. Of course, I strongly believe that no creation in this world can be totally original. Only the percentage of creativity will be more in one and less in another. Even the greatest of poets, artists, and writers and so on get their inspiration from nature, incidents and people around them. Even the age old saints of India who gave the eternal knowledge as *Vedas* were humble enough to proclaim that they received the great knowledge through vibrations from space during their supra conscious meditative state. But it is not enough if one has mere interest or persistence. One should also have the necessary capacity. You know very well that I can sing. But if I try to imitate a great singer how ridiculous it will be? Suppose I try to become witty and humorous like any good humorist then I will only make the others laugh at me instead of I making them laugh. So one must know one's strengths and weaknesses and act accordingly. Otherwise he will become a laughing stock only".

"O K. All that I wanted to say is please try once for my sake. I am not asking you to imitate any one. That is of no good. Imitation can never turn out to be original. You may create your own style of writing. Think that you are writing this book specially for me only. Anyway, I leave it to you. You do as you wish".

By that time all had finished their lunch. It was also time for my husband and me to get ready for our journey. So we both put a full stop to our discussion and finished our lunch quickly.

As I was thinking about all these I began to doze off and my husband who was engaged in conversation with the one who was sitting opposite to him on the side seat came to me and said, "This lower birth is allotted to that *Swamiji*. He has agreed to go to the upper birth". We were allotted the upper births. It is then that I actually noticed the person who was sitting opposite to my husband. He was wearing a saffron robe and his countenance revealed his inner tranquility and clarity. My husband introduced me to that *Sanyasi*, the monk and I thanked him for his act of kindness in allowing me to have the lower birth. My husband then said "This *Swamiji* is a doctor by profession. He is returning after visiting very many temples and places and very many sages in the north particularly in the Himalayan regions. He is narrating all his experiences there and also about some of the teachings of those spiritual masters". I wished I could also listen to him. But he was talking in a very low tone that was audible only to the person who was sitting close by. The two children who were sitting opposite to me were also making a hell of a noise that his voice got drowned in that chaos and I could only hear some words of his here and there although I was eager to listen to all that he was saying.

The train reached the *Katpadi* junction. I took out the dinner packets and water from the bag, took out a paper plate and after putting a few *Chappathis* and curry on that plate I offered it to the *Swamiji*. But after expressing his thankfulness with all humility, with folded hands he said "Thanks a lot. But I take only some fruits or a cup of milk in the night- that too not always but only rarely. Kindly excuse me for not accepting the food that you offered. Let me see whether I can get some fruits or milk here. Even if nothing is available it is perfectly all right for me because I am not at all particular about food. Only when I feel hungry I take something". Saying this he got up and went towards the door. The family with the two children also took out their dinner packets and the mother after feeding the younger one and serving food to the older one and her husband finally started eating. After their dinner the children again continued with their play and fights.

As soon as we finished our dinner the phone rang. I knew that it must be our son. After we left the *Tirupathi* station he has phoned to us twice and this is the third time he is calling us. Every time our daughter in law and the kids also spoke to us. The younger one innocently enquired whether we reached *Kerala*. The elder one wanted to know how we are enjoying our journey.

Our son asked, "Where are you now? Has the train reached *Katpadi* junction? Did you have your dinner? He went on.

"Yes. The train has reached *Katpadi* a couple of minutes ago and just now we finished our dinner. Both of us are enjoying the journey thoroughly. Tell *Roopa* (our daughter-in-law) that her *chappathis* and the curry are excellent and quite tasty. What about children? Have they gone to bed? It is so silent there. I am not hearing the children making noise".

"Both of them have finished their dinner and are watching some cartoon Channel in the T V and we are having our dinner now".

"All right. We will call you tomorrow morning as soon as we reach *Palakkad.* Take care. Good night".

"Take care. Good night."

My husband said that he is not feeling sleepy and provided the *Swamiji* is willing he would like to listen to him for some more time. The train began to leave the station and the *Swamiji* returned to his seat. "Could you get anything?" asked my husband. "Yes I could get a cup of milk" he said.

"Usually at what time do you go to bed?" asked my husband.

"I have no fixed time for that. I go to bed only when I feel sleepy. Sometimes I sit and read some books the whole night".

Although I was also not feeling sleepy I spread out the blanket and the sheets that the Railways gave us and I stretched myself on that. Again my mind began to wander. This time the thought was about my new book.

I thought , may be, this *Swamiji* can help me and provide me with some information that I required for my new book 'The Art of Peaceful and Happy Living' because, peace and happiness one can achieve only by removing negativity in oneself by following righteous, and ethical paths that are stressed by religion and spirituality. But how can I present the facts through my creative thinking and how can I give a touch of fiction there? But then I thought, how did the sages compose *Puranas* and the *Ithihasas* or epics? Did not the sages convey the lofty eternal truths of the *Vedas* through innumerable simple tales in *Puranas* and *Ithihasas*? So that means it is possible. So why can't I also convey the ideas that I wanted to present in my book in the form of some fictitious story or something similar to that?

Such thoughts made me weave out a small story first. I tried, but nothing seemed to materialize. Although I could remember certain incidents in my life that could be molded in to some story still I began to grope in the dark when I came to the point of connecting it with the subject matter of my new book that is the 'Best possible life'.

Then suddenly my mind went back to the story that I wrote several years ago when I was a student in the college. I wrote the story to the best of my ability with the desire and intention to contribute it to the college magazine. As a student I allowed no stone unturned. I participated in all curricular, co-curricular activities, and sports and games. I put my heart and soul in to everything that I had my hands on. However writing a story for the college magazine was my first attempt in writing. I always considered myself as Jack of all trades but master in none as I seem to be interested in everything. Although I did write a story I didn't have the courage and confidence to submit it to my teacher who was put in-charge of the college magazine. I also did not tell anything about my attempt to anyone. But now I thought that the story did convey the truth that one should always become the master of one's mind because the mind that is profoundly powerful is also quite dangerous as a single slip in our thoughts can ruin our entire life. Definitely it has some connection with what I intended to write in my new book. Then I started remembering the story though not fully, and the story in a nutshell went on like this.

The unreserved compartment of the train was over crowded with passengers. The passengers were standing all over the place, even in between the seats and all through the passage up to the door. It was a midsummer night and the atmosphere was very sultry both outside and more so inside the compartment and almost all those who were lucky enough to get a little space to sit were dozing off. Those who were standing by squeezing themselves in the available space had no choice except to be awake although they felt sleepy as the train sped with a rhythmic sound. Any rhythmic sound induced sleep. Perhaps it was the rhythmic sound of the heartbeat of the mother and that of the baby inside her that induced sleep in the child even before the child was born. This instinct man carried up to his grave. As it was a passenger train it stopped at each and every small station.

One old man was sitting on the doorstep and seeing a youngster standing by his side, he moved as far he could and offered some space to the youngster to sit there along with him. With a look of gratitude the youngster sat near him. From their attire it was very clear that both of them were living in poverty. The old man then offered a *bidi* to the youngster and he in turn took it with a smile and thankfulness .The old man also offered him a match stick to light the *bidi.*

"Where are you going?" asked the old man.

"I am going to one of my relative's place. This is the first time I am coming to this area. How far is the station X from here?"

"Oh, I see. So you are new to this place. It will be another 30 minutes before the train reaches that station. Don't worry. I will tell you when the train reaches that station".

"Are you also getting down there?"

"No, no. But I belong to this area only. I am not getting down there.'

The train was passing through a forest. The youngster then asked the other, "Does this forest contain wild animals?"

"No no. not at all. The people of nearby villages come over here to fetch fire wood for their family". Suddenly with a distant look in his eyes and in a thoughtful mood he said "There was a man living in one of the nearby villages here. He belonged to that place where you are going."

"I see. But what is so special about him that you are mentioning and remembering him now at this hour"?

"See, His life was so special that none can forget him."

"Is he alive now or dead?

"Nobody knows whether he is alive now or not. His name was *Ratnagar*. He was born and brought up in the village and he also got married to his cousin belonging to the same village. The couple had two little children, one girl and another younger one who was a boy. Both *Ratnagar* and his wife were very good and virtuous. Years passed and *Ratnagar's* daughter who was married now to a distant relative of his was living with her in-laws in the same village. They had a small girl child who was nearly two years old. *Ratnagar*'s son who was by now a youngster was doing a small business in the village itself. *Ratnagar*, his wife and their son were staying in their old hut.

One day a friend of *Ratnagar* happened to visit him. He was employed as a worker in a business establishment in the nearby town. He told *Ratnagar* that one of the richest business men of that place who happened to be the friend of his master was in need of a gardener who can also be a watchman for his house as the one who was working as gardener in their house had left the job and gone back to his native place as he became very old. He wanted an honest and committed person for that work and he was prepared to offer an attractive salary as money was not a problem for him. *Ratnagar's* friend wanted to know whether *Ratnagar* was willing to go there. *Ratnagar* thought for a while and he told his friend that he will tell his decision the next day. At home he consulted this matter with his wife and son and as *Ratnagar* was willing to take up that work his wife and son also gave their consent. The very next day *Ratnagar* went to the house of his friend and told him his willingness to accept the job.

It was nearly five years since *Ratnagar* had been working in that house. His honesty, sincerity and commitment towards his work made everyone in the house like him very much. Soon he became a part of the family. His master, his wife and their little child, *Ramya*, who was nearly four years old, became so fond of him that he became indispensable in the house. *Ratnagar* visited his house every month and spent two days with his family. He took his entire salary and gave it to his wife as all his needs were met by the master himself. Whatever extra money he got during festivals and on special occasions he kept with himself for his own small and sundry expenses. He also saved some portion of that and bought some gifts particularly for his grandchild and also for all the other members of his family. He gave the gifts to them when he visited his home every month.

One day as usual *Ratnagar* was watering the plants in the garden in the morning. After watering all the plants he began to wipe and clean the two cars that were kept in the portico of the house. *Ramya*, his master's little daughter came running to him and offered him a lot of chocolates as it was her birthday. The child was wearing a costly new dress and glittering gold and diamond jewels. *Ratnagar* while receiving the chocolates from her got a glimpse of all those jewels that she was wearing. Instantaneously he remembered his granddaughter. Suddenly the devil took possession of him and he began to think "What is the use of being honest and virtuous in this world? My honesty and sincerity has brought nothing except poverty to me. What could I do for my wife and children all these years except that I could provide them simple food every day that was just sufficient for them? If only I can buy at least one small gold chain for my grandchild how happy will be my wife and daughter? But then where will I go for the money? I don't think I can ever afford to buy even a bit of gold to my grandchild. What if I take just one chain that this little child is wearing and give it as my gift to my grandchild? My daughter also will be very happy. I shall tell my wife and daughter that I bought the jewels. After all, it won't be a big loss for my master. But what will happen when they come to know about it? Any way they will never suspect me as I have been very honest all these years". All these thoughts began to come one after the other in his mind. At that moment he forgot all those virtues that he was following till then in his life. He took the child to a corner of the compound and told her,

"Shall I show you a magic?

The child, who was very affectionate towards *Ratnagar*, asked him innocently and eagerly, "What magic?"

"See, I am going to remove some of your jewels one after the other and I will tie them in my towel. Then I will utter some *Mantra* for some seconds. When I untie the towel you will see all new jewels that are more beautiful than the ones that you are wearing now, and you can have the new ornaments in the place of the old ones."

The little child believed all that *Ratnagar* said.

At that moment when *Ratnagar* was about to remove her jewels her father came out of the house calling her. "*Ramya, Ramya*, where are you? We have to go to the temple now. It is already late".

Before the child could reply, without knowing what he is doing *Ratnagar* shut her mouth so that his master will not come to know of his act. In fear *Ramya* began to struggle to release herself and as she tried *Ratnagar* began to shut her mouth more tightly, may be along with her nose as well. This made the child breathless and she fell down. *Ratnagar* for a moment lost all his senses. He did not know what to do. He knew that he killed the girl though not intentionally. His face became pale with fear and shame and his whole body trembled. The panic stricken *Ratnagar* ran for his life and soon he got into a bus and finally reached home in a dazed condition that evening.

When *Ratnagar*'s wife saw him she was surprised. Only two days back he visited his family with his pay packet and a few gifts as usual. When she looked at the face of *Ratnagar* she could assess that something had gone wrong with him. She at once asked "What's wrong with you? Why are you looking so pale? Are you not all right?" Without saying even a single word *Ratnagar* sat in a corner of that single room hut silently. His wife gave him a glass of water immediately and asked him to drink it. She asked him to relax for some time. Again she continued, "What's wrong with you? I am going on asking you and without telling me anything you are looking at the street in fright. Tell me what happened. Why are you sitting like this as if you have lost everything? *Ratnagar* continued to look outside towards the street in great fear as he expected the police to arrest him any moment. After some moments he regained his balance and narrated to her in a choked voice full of guilt and fear all that had happened that morning. However he did not tell her about the fate of the child as a result of his act.

All on a sudden his wife began to cry aloud and said "What have you done? How did you have the heart to cheat your master who was so kind to you and act in such a manner towards the child who was so fond of you? If we are poor that is because we have done something wrong before. We are only reaping the effect of that. Even though we are poor didn't we live happily all these years without deviating from our righteous path? Which devil enter into your mind and overpower you? Go at once to your master and admit your evil intention and seek his pardon. Even if he removes you from your job it does not matter at all. God will show us some path or the other. He will never let us down. Did you think I would appreciate you and become happy if you had brought the child's ornaments? Why should we crave for anybody else's possessions? What peace of mind and happiness we can have by that? Return immediately and apologize for what you have done and seek the pardon of your master. Let us wash off the sin of your act at least in that manner".

Ratnagar at once got up and went out. He was in a fix. How could he seek the pardon of his master? Who will ever pardon the killer of his only little daughter? *Ratnagar* could not return to his master. He walked and walked and soon he realized that he was nearing the railway station. A train was nearing the station. At once he ran in to the station, bought a ticket hurriedly and somehow got in to the moving train that was leaving the station slowly.

Days, months and years rolled on. *Ratnagar* the wanderer never returned home. He earned a living by working wherever he went. But the guilt of his wrong deed never left him. It was always pricking his mind. He lost all happiness and peace of mind. As a penance he led the life of a monk sacrificing even his need for food most of the time. Whatever he earned more than what he needed to maintain his body he gave it to the old and helpless people who were poorer than him. He very much wanted to return home; but he had no guts to face his wife and children. Perhaps the police had come in search of him and his wife would have come to know the fate of the child also. What would have been their feeling when they had come to know that he killed the child? All these thoughts always made him more restless and unhappy. He became a wretched man.

One day suddenly he began to think "did the child actually fall down dead? After all as far as I can remember I only shut her mouth but not her nose. She might have only swooned with fear; but how to know about this?" *Ratnagar* cursed himself for not trying to find out what happened to that child afterwards. Now recollecting the whole incident scene by scene he clearly remembered that he has not made the child breathless. This thought urged him to find out the truth.

Ratnagar reached the place where he was working. It was morning time. Nobody could recognize him as he was dressed shabbily and had become a totally shattered man by now. He stood under a tree near the house of the master. Soon he saw the car of his master coming out of the house and a teenage girl was sitting in a school uniform by the side of his master who was driving the car. At once he knew that it was none other than the same child *Ramya*, the only daughter of his master. Some untold joy and happiness engulfed *Ratnagar's* body and mind totally. He forgot himself for a moment. Such was his joy. He would not have experienced such joy even if he had got the entire wealth of the universe. He also felt very much relieved of a heavy burden that was causing him immense torture all these years. "Why didn't I try to find out the truth till now? Why did the thought come to me only now? Was it because I had to suffer till today for my mean and unfaithful and ungrateful thought?"

All on a sudden *Ratnagar* became a new man. He was feeling very much relieved from the thought that he was a murderer. However the guilt of his wrong thoughts continued to haunt him. For a split second he thought "Why not I go back to my family? But then how will my wife and son receive me now after so many years? How can they show the same love and affection towards me as before?" Finally *Ratnagar* decided not to return to his village at all. He was not as dejected and depressed a man as before. However a feeling of total detachment came to him-detachment that was born out of his frustration in the beginning stages and acceptance later in course of time that taught him to endure everything patiently without any complaints or self-pity.

The train stopped. The old man told the youngster "Your station has come".

While getting down from the train the youngster asked eagerly "What happened to *Ratnagar* after that?

The old man replied "Nobody knows what happened to him later. Anyway, wish you a happy time with your relatives".

By then the train started moving and *Ratnagar* who was looking at the distant huts muttered to himself, "My friend, how could you not make out that, that *Ratnagnar* was none other but myself? How could I explain about all that had happened in his life in such a detailed manner if I am not the same *Ratnagar*? Dear friend, any way thank you very much for giving me the opportunity to tell my sad story. Oh God thank you, tonight I could tell another man the story of my life that would make him realize how a man's life can be shattered by a split second vicious thought and how his life would have been otherwise if only he had followed the virtuous path that could have definitely resulted in making his life the most beautiful, happy, peaceful and blessed. Oh, my God, let me atone for my sin at least this way". With all these thoughts in his mind, *Ratnagar* looked intently at a particular hut that was not far away from the railway line and the silhouette of which was dimly visible in the moon light. Without shifting his eyes from the sight he fondly remembered the good old happy days that he spent with his family in that small little hut and the train began to gain speed as it left the limits of the station.

As the two children were fast asleep by now, I could hear the words of that *Sanyasi* very clearly. Though I was feeling quite sleepy now, still, I began concentrating on what he was saying. As sleep was overtaking me now I could hear him only intermittently.

2

Peace and Happiness through Best Possible Life

"Swamiji, Will you please spare some time for clearing my doubts"? I asked.

With a smile he said, "Why not? As far as I can, I will definitely answer you"

"Swamiji, why do we see duality, I mean, good and bad in this world? Can man do away with such duality? Why can't man choose only the good leaving all that are termed as bad? Is it possible for man to achieve the best life? If not what is the best possible life that he can achieve? What should we do for achieving Peace and Happiness in life? How can one eliminate one's negativity and generate positivity in him?" I went on.

"Wait, wait; you are seeking answers for very many questions at the same time. Let me try to answer all your questions. But kindly put your questions one by one. Otherwise my answers will look like a monologue or a sermon".

"O K, Swamiji, let me put it like this. Why should good and bad exist together in this world? Can't we do away with the dualities of life"?

"See, duality is the very basis of life. It is the very basis of creation itself. This is what we experience in our life. God and the devil, good and the bad, the divine and the demon, the hero and the villain, positive and negative are in the very nature of life and that of the world we live in. They are like the two sides of the same coin. Even if we crave to have only the good, the positive and the divine it cannot become a reality for us because both good and bad, positive and negative co-exist in this world. Only their proportions will differ. Either what we call the good or the positive will be more or less in one or in one situation or the bad or the negative will be more or less in another or in another situation. This is because duality is the very basis of all creation whether it is with the beings or the cosmos itself."

"According to the ancient Indian thinking before the creation of the universe everything was one, single energy –the Absolute energy- This the ancient Indian *Rishis* or the sages denoted as the *Purusha* or *Parabhrahmam or Paramatma*, or the *Chaitanya*, the Absolute energy, or the Absolute soul or the Absolute Consciousness. The same notion is expressed by the modern cosmogonists though in different terms. Scientists also state that the universe erupted from a primordial singular point known as Singularity and the universe with about the 100 billion galaxies containing about 100 billion stars stretching out more than about 10 billion light years in all directions was once squeezed into an infinitesimally small space far smaller than a single electron". It is like the seed that contains a big tree in itself.

"According to the ancient Indian view before the creation of the cosmos this Absolute, supreme energy was single, unique and undifferentiated. But it contained in itself in potential form *Prakruthi* or nature or matter within itself. When *Purusha* the Absolute Energy contained *Prakruthi* or matter in itself in a hidden, undifferentiated manner, then there was no creation. At that time *Prakruthi* was in a balanced state. That means all the three qualities of Nature or *Prakruthi* namely, *Satva* (Purity), *Rajas* (Passion) and *Tamasic* (Ignorance and delusion) retained their equilibrium. But when this balance was disturbed due to the play of the factor 'Time' then there was imbalance in Nature as one or the other quality or qualities of Nature or *Prakruthi* became more pronounced or visible than the other or other two qualities and *Prakruthi* or nature or matter got differentiated from *Purusha*, the Absolute, or the energy, and what was one before as Absolute became identified as two, the *Purusha* the Absolute or the Energy and *Prakruthi*, the nature or matter and this was the starting point of duality. When *Prakruthi* got manifested and pronounced, it gave rise to the creation of the universe and the objects and beings with varied names and forms that was full of duality. So duality was born along with the creation of the universe and beings and no one can ignore it or avoid it in material worldly life".

"*How can one achieve maximum peace and happiness in one's life*"? I asked him again.

"While the entire positive or what we call as good leads to happiness and peace for man, all that we call bad or negative results in misery and unhappiness to one all and this is the fact of life. But all beings in the world crave only for happiness and peace. Peace and happiness are interdependent and they appear together. When there is peace then there is happiness and when there is happiness that means there is peace inside us. Happiness is the outcome of peace and peace is the result of inner happiness in man. One who is unhappy will always be disturbed inside without peace of mind. But then peace results only when there is inner tranquility. When we are able to find peace within us then we can live at peace with others. Both happiness and peace bring about a glow on our face and tranquility in our heart. Peace can come only from within and it is the result of minimizing negativity and maximizing positivity in one. Nobody on earth wants unhappiness or misery. When that is the case how can we achieve maximum happiness and peace during our life? When we know fully well that we cannot do away with duality completely in the world, then is it possible to eliminate all negativity and to have only positivity? It is not. If only we can eliminate the weeds of negativity totally by plucking their very roots, it is possible. But then the remnants of the weeds will always be there and the best possible that one can do is to be in constant alert to see that we remove the weeds as soon as they sprout.

Removing all weeds totally and permanently without any further scope for them to grow and filling the entire landscape with only good useful plants that one wants to grow, though not impossible is an extremely difficult task. So also filling one's mind with only positivity without the slightest traces of negativity as it is very difficult for a normal worldly man. However we can plant as many positive thoughts as is possible for us. If we can do that then we will realize that every time we create at least one positive thought it pays huge dividends to us in the form of peace and happiness and this will encourage us to increase our positivity that will ensure us more and more happiness and peace."

"Swamiji, in the epics we come across the stories of sages who had exhibited anger in the form of uttering curses. That means even they, who had transformed and elevated their minds were not exceptions to this negativity in their mind. When that is the case with the enlightened souls, then what about we, the ordinary humans?"

"The great *Rishis* or the sages of the past who were spiritually highly evolved and who were the personification of *Vijnana* or spiritual wisdom exhibited anger outwardly even though they never had any such emotion deep inside their mind, because they were the masters of their mind. They could manipulate and direct their mind and the thoughts the way they desired. Their mind was their servant not master. They were not unconscious of their outward negativity. They intentionally, consciously brought out what appeared to be negative outwardly and they directed their negative energy the way they wanted. In many instances their expression of negativity, for example, in the form of curses as a result of their outward anger was meant only for the welfare of mankind. There was no selfish motive in that act although utterances of curses by the great sages made the common man in his ignorance to believe that they were really angry when anyone acted against their will or when one did not show due respect to them in the proper manner. This is because the sages made use of different techniques to transform people who acted as per their *Samskaras* or accumulated tendencies of their long past and their conditioning in their present life. To elevate the minds of the people the *Rishis* had to resort to various means like uttering curses, or instilling fear in the minds of the people whose ignorance of reality was very high. It is like the mother showing her sense of displeasure or anger to her dear child. The end was to make the child a good human being. With that end in view she resorts to various means which may seem to be harsh or negative to the child. We on the other hand create and project negativity as a result of our very nature; because of our ego sense, expectations, desire, and attachments and so on. So there is a lot of difference between the negativity that is exhibited by the great souls and that of ordinary humans".

"Swamiji, in today's world negativity seems to have taken an upper hand over positivity. When that is the case how to overpower the negativity that is the source of all unhappiness and misery in the world, so that man leads a life of happiness and peace in the midst of all the challenges, failures, demands, and disappointments and so on of life?"

"If a man wants to live and die happily and peacefully which is the ultimate goal and objective of life itself then the only way is to be fully conscious and alert and wakeful to all his thoughts, words and actions, be fully aware of them, understand them in an unbiased manner like a witness and allow and command his mind to take control of such negativity so that it is not allowed to grow in his mind. Simultaneously he should fill his mind instantaneously with the necessary good and positive thoughts, words and deeds. If he is sincere, honest, committed and persistent in his efforts then he is sure to increase positivity remarkably and reduce his negativity that harm and destroy his very life and that of the others. Gradually he will be able to become more and more positive in his thoughts, feelings, words and actions. If a man can do this much then he is sure to make his life worthy, purposeful, blissful and peaceful. In the entire creation, this craving for permanent peace and happiness is unique to human beings only but not to other lower species of creations".

"Swamiji, is man the only being in this creation who is endowed with consciousness that is awareness and is he the only being seeking permanent peace and happiness"?

"Consciousness in the sense of awareness is present in the entire creation because the source of all creation is the same. But grosser the creation the less pronounced is the level of consciousness. It is in gradation as we progress from mountains, land, oceans, insects, reptiles, birds, animals and humans. So while the level of consciousness is highly pronounced in man gradually it becomes more and more submerged in other lower levels of creations. Every being in this creation has intelligence, emotions and so on. They too derive happiness and undergo suffering, pain and sorrow at least in a temporary manner. This may not be visible in the case of highly gross things like mountains but is visible to a certain extent in the case of plants and is more visible in the case of animals. In the lowest levels of creation like mountains the consciousness is very much submerged and not pronounced. But even here it has been found that the Himalaya is growing. As we move up in the ladder of creation we see consciousness becoming more and more pronounced. Rivers take their own course to flow. A creeper tends to grow towards its support so that it can hold on to it and grow. Plants turn towards sunlight for their growth and so on. It is said that trees get tensed when they are about to be cut. The level of consciousness that is visible in animals is more than what is seen in plants and trees and so on. An insect like ant gets attracted towards a place where there is sugar but not salt. Birds also build nests to lay their eggs and protect their little ones".

"In the case of birds and animals the consciousness level is limited to their survival and the instinct of reproduction. It is limited to achieving temporary happiness by appeasing their thirst and hunger and fulfilling their desire for sleep and rest, and procreation. No doubt man too has these two basic needs or desires that are found in the animals namely, the appeasement of hunger, thirst, sleep and rest and the instinct of procreation and reproduction that are to be fulfilled in his life and they are to be fulfilled. It is only natural. But man as the higher species of creation is endowed with a higher and subtler level of intelligence and capacity to discriminate good from bad, and unlike the other lower species he is also endowed with higher and greater capacity and freedom to mold his life the way he wants. Also man has innumerable desires, likes and dislikes. But while the lower species of life desire for only temporary happiness man by being the highest species in the order of creation, wants happiness and peace not only temporarily but also permanently. Only man can derive permanent happiness that can be termed as Bliss or *Ananda* that has no opposite and hence any duality. He can achieve permanent happiness and peace by knowing his mind, by transforming his mind that is by elevating his mind to a higher dimension and finally by transcending his mind that is going beyond his mind. He is endowed with the freedom either to choose a life that is purposeful, worthy, beneficial, happy and peaceful or make his life unhappy, miserable, purposeless, and unworthy for himself and his fellow beings. The choice is ours. And the universal truth is that man always wants to make his life purposeful, worthy, happy, beneficial and peaceful. To achieve this collective end he struggles. But the pity is that, most people do not understand that to achieve this goal one should make the right choices in one's life and sincerely and honestly work towards it. As the age old proverb goes what we sow we reap. What we give we get".

"Just as one seed gives rise to a big tree that yields innumerable seeds through its fruits similarly one single negative thought, word or deed will also result in multifold negative tendencies in our mind in course of time. Similarly one single positive thought may result in innumerable positive thoughts, words and deeds in one. While the negative tendencies ruin one and also spread negativity everywhere around that person, the positive tendencies elevate one mentally resulting in his mental happiness and peace and they also spread positivity everywhere and make those around him happy and peaceful as well".

"Can anyone become a personification of all that are good, and all that are positive in this world? Can he become totally good and positive in all his thoughts, feelings, words and deeds"?

"Actually only the one who goes beyond all dualities of life, who is purity personified can become totally positive. It is not because he wants to be positive. It is because total positivity that is purity becomes his very nature. Such a one is detached from the worldly life both physically as well as mentally because he becomes one who has reached a different dimension altogether. Such a one is beyond the sense of ego, desires and attachments of life. So nothing in this world is either good or bad for him but only pure. Such a one is bound to be a personification of all that we term as good or positive".

"As I said, in the world there are both good as well as bad, both negative as well as positive. It is like a cinema that has the hero, the villain, the good and positive situations as well as bad situations. We are able to know the good because there is the bad as well. It is the very spice of life. Good and bad, positivity and negativity are inevitable in the world. But then man does not want unhappiness or misery that is the outcome of bad and negative. He wants only peace and happiness always. To achieve this he must be devoid of all negativity and instead have only positivity in him. But then he cannot ignore or avoid the very basis of life, namely duality. He cannot make the world devoid of all negativity either in himself or in others or in situations. But he can sincerely work with persistence to make himself good and positive up to his maximum ability as he cannot change the nature of the world, the persons outside himself and situations. He has to bring out the necessary changes in himself because that is the only thing that is under his own control. If he can do this much then he can make his life the best possible if not the best one because it is impossible for ordinary humans who is worldly and who is in the midst of all challenges and responsibilities of life to attain the best, to have the best life with only positive and good thoughts, feelings, words and deeds without the slightest traces of negativity.

No doubt, the best life is the ideal but an ideal is always an ideal. Even if one can make one's life the best possible then that itself is a very great achievement. On the other hand one should know that there were and are great souls many of whom are unknown, who have made their life the best. So it means that the best, the ideal life is not impossible but humanly possible. But one should choose the life of a saint who has renounced the worldly life to achieve that goal. For all worldly people who lead a normal life with all the desires and ambitions of life with all the challenges that they have to face in life, with all the duties and responsibilities that they have to fulfill in performing their role in life in the best possible manner, it becomes highly impossible to feel, think, speak and act positively in an honest manner all the time without any hypocrisy.

The householder who leads a normal worldly life is not as free as a saint not only because he has very many duties and responsibilities but because he is also one who has the sense of ego in himself, the desires and attachments to objects, places, people and so on. Hence the possibility of a life that is best possible but not the best for men who lead a normal worldly life. Even if he is able to make his life the best possible, it is great. Once he makes his life the best possible then his journey towards achieving the best life will not be far off. He will be able to reach that stage automatically in course of time".

"Why can't one aim for the best life instead of the best possible life, Swamiji?"

"Anyone who puts in the required effort to improve himself can aspire for the best life. It is not wrong. But he cannot be certain of reaching that goal in the present birth itself. This is because of his limitations as a worldly person and his inherent accumulated tendencies. When he sets a certain target, the result, then there is every possibility that he may become disheartened, if he fails to reach the target even after continuous persistent efforts.

If a good student aims for the first rank then it may be possible for him to achieve that goal because he has been continuously a good student who has understood the subject thoroughly and if he puts in his best efforts there is every possibility that he can achieve that goal. But if a student who has been continuously poor in his studies or is below average in his studies aims for the first rank in the examination then it is not easy for him. He has to put in immense efforts and he may even have to skip the examinations that year so that he prepares himself thoroughly from the start and write the exams the next year so that he becomes worthy and eligible for getting the first rank in the examination. Similarly one who is an average person with many positive and negatives in him cannot easily replace all his negativity and have all positivity. It is also a fact that man carries all his accumulated impressions of the past even at his very birth. After his birth his character is shaped and influenced and conditioned by several other factors, like his parents, family surroundings, teachers, friends, the existing social, political set up, and so on. Each of these factors plays a role in molding his character. His character becomes a combination of all these factors and he becomes conditioned in one way or the other. It is not easy for anyone to ignore and throw away or discard all these factors that determine one's nature. However it is humanly possible.

Even the one who is full of negativity can make himself in to new human being so that he becomes an ideal person with all positivity only. This is possible with knowledge about the harmful effects of negativity, awareness and proper understanding of one's own negative temperaments, the will and determination to change oneself and a persistent and continuous effort in creating and strengthening positivity in one that will overcome all one's present belief systems, conditioning of oneself and the accumulated *Samskaras* that make the one what he is. So even in the same birth one can achieve the best life provided he can become the best. In the great epic *Ramayana* we come across the life story of *Ratnakaran* the dacoit who became the great sage *Valmiki* , the *Adi Kavi* who wrote the *Adi Kavya* namely *Ramayana*".

"When one is able to practise all virtues to the fullest extent then he becomes what he actually is- a pure soul. But normally this is not possible for an ordinary worldly person who has very many duties and responsibilities to perform. Such a person cannot become an embodiment of all virtues because of his limitations. A man who leads a worldly life also cannot fully do what is expected of him to the fullest extent because of many of his limitations. What is good for one may also not be good for the other. He can at the most be the best in a few relationships or he can perform in an average manner so that he tries to fulfill all his varied duties, for example, as a son, as a husband, as a father, as an employee or employer, as a social being and so on to the best of his ability. Even if he tries his very best he will only be able to fulfill his varied duties up to a certain extent only . That means he can't make everyone around him happy to the same extent. So, if he is able to make his life the best possible that itself is a great thing. Once he is able to achieve this automatically he will become purer and purer and will be able to achieve the best life".

"What is meant by going beyond good and bad, Swamiji"?

"As I have already pointed out both good and bad exist only for worldly people because these belong to the body and mind with which the ordinary worldly people associate themselves with. Whatever is desirable for the body and mind we call it good and whatever is undesirable for our body and mind we categorize them as bad. When anything leads to physical ill health we consider that as bad for our body and whatever we perceive as bad and results in unhappiness and misery thereby cause mental ill health we consider as bad. When everything goes on as per our expectations then we consider it as good and we become happy. On the other hand if it is the reverse then we consider it as bad as it gives us unhappiness. In real life we cannot have everything as per our expectations because we have no control over those that are external to us whether they are objects, people or situations. But the ultimate objective of all worldly people is to have and enjoy a happy and peaceful life. For this purpose one tries to generate and practice all virtues if possible or at least as many virtues as possible for him so that he will have only the least negativity in him. Such a life is termed as *Dharmic* way of living or the righteous way of living and the virtues that are practiced are called as *Dharmas* in Sanskrit. Such a life becomes possible when one through self-analysis is able to know the mind and transform the mind from its lower level that contains negativity to a higher level that imbibes positive values. We know positivity generates more and more positivity in us. The tendencies of such a person who follows the righteous path will be highly positive and good and he will reap what he has sown. He is bound to get what he gave. That means he will have to be born again to enjoy the fruits of his past positive *Karmas* or actions and this will go on and on resulting in repeated births and deaths for such a person".

"But when one becomes spiritually elevated he not only understands his mind and transforms his mind through self-enquiry but he is also able to transcend his mind through his spiritual knowledge. Such a one realizes that he is actually neither the body nor the mind but is only pure consciousness, the soul. He does not bother about what is good or bad for his body or mind because to him he is neither the body nor mind but is the pure inner spirit, the consciousness that is not affected by any good or bad that we, the ordinary people perceive in this world. The worldly life looks as a child's play for him and be becomes disinterested in such a play. At such a stage one becomes totally soul conscious and he detaches himself and becomes indifferent to the consequences of all worldly activities that he has to perform as a human being. Whatever he does is for the welfare of all. Without any expectation of the results and without the sense of doership and by dedicating all his works to the supreme spirit, the Absolute consciousness that pervades the entire cosmos, he acts. Such a one goes beyond all positive and negative, good and bad because he goes beyond all dualities of life knowing fully well that any duality is caused because of our perception of anything as good or bad that influences our body and mind that are only our outer and inner instruments but not the real self. He does not get affected by any of the dualities of life because he does not get entangled in them or get stuck in them. The good and bad in life do not affect him because he views them as natural happenings in life. Whatever comes to him whether it is good or bad he accepts them in an impartial manner. This does not mean that he becomes like a machine without any feelings or emotions.

Arjuna who listened to the entire discourse of *Bhagavadgita* from the very mouth of Lord Krishna could not control his emotions and he became a totally shattered man on hearing the death of *Abhimanyu*, his son in the war. However he regained his mental stability and took part in the warfare as before with a steady mind. That means he did not allow his mind to become weak, instead he took control of his emotions and feelings with the knowledge that was imparted to him by the Lord.

The revelation and the knowledge that we are not the body or mind but the imperishable Atman makes one a mere witness or an observer of everything that is going on in this world without entangling himself in any of the play of body and that of the mind. In the case of such elevated souls, whatever they think, speak and do will only be good because they are essentially pure. They think, speak and do good not because they are good, not because that will enable them to become happy and peaceful, and not because their goodness will be rewarded, but because it is their very nature to do good. If the mother loves her child, especially the newborn then it is because that love flows out of her naturally. There is no selfish motive or expectation in that. Positivity becomes the very nature of spiritually elevated souls. Such a person who goes beyond good and bad frees himself from the entanglement of the continuous process of births and deaths and thereby gets liberated. This becomes possible when one transcends the mind and becomes an embodiment of purity. Such a person goes beyond all dualities, all good and bad of life".

"When negativity ruins the very life of man is it not advisable that we make children understand the necessity of eliminating negativity in them even when they are young, so that they lead a life of happiness and peace later when they grow up and make their life purposeful and worthy? What is the role of parents and teachers in this?"

"Even among children we find some children more friendly and accommodative and tolerant. These children also like to share their toys and other things with other children, they attract more and more friends and they are liked by each and every one. On the other hand there are children, who always engage in fighting, not sharing and also jealous of the other children. This is because of their inherent nature that is based upon their past accumulated tendencies. These tendencies get more and more deep rooted and intensified as they grow older. Extreme competitive spirit is another factor that leads to more and more negativity in children. This leads to unnecessary comparisons and comparisons are always onerous. In the modern world children are extremely burdened with this".

"First of all the positive tendencies in children should be noticed by the parents and teachers and they must do everything they can to strengthen that. The parents and teachers through proper counseling should make the children understand the greatness, importance and benefits of positivity so that the children follow the virtues on their own accord. Similarly whenever any negative is noticed in children they must be made to understand the harmful consequences of their negativity through proper counseling. The parents and teachers should constantly watch the behavior of children for detecting any negative tendency in them and the reasons for that. Any negative tendency that they notice in children should be tackled in a friendly, loving and affectionate manner. For example if a child is found to be dishonest then he should not be chided or punished or ridiculed especially in front of others. A loving and affectionate conversation with the child after taking him in to confidence will enable the parents and teachers to find out the root cause for such a behavior on his part and after making him understand the harmful effects of such a tendency they can help the child to tackle and get over such problems, such negativities.

Merely scolding and punishing children especially in front of other children and grownups for any negativity found in them will only make them more and more depressed, stressed, anxious, diffident, unhappy and worried and so on. This will also create fear and low self-esteem in them and also hatred and contempt and so on and the children will not be able to put forth their best. Such punishments may even make children moody, unsocial and even anti-social as they grow up because they develop a sense of hatred towards all in course of time".

"The parents and teachers can generate positive qualities in children only when they themselves have the required character. It is not enough if they pay attention to the physical needs and development of the children and their intellectual development and achievements. More importantly they should take care of the psychological or the emotional development of children. Mere preaching will not have any effect on children because little children try to imitate the parents and teachers in an unconscious manner. In good old days we had 'Moral instruction' as one of the subjects. That seemed to be absent in schools of today. I wish all the schools have this subject on par with the other subjects. It is not enough if our children are able to master the subjects that give them material success later. They should become good human beings first."

"Most of the modern parents feel that the lack of competitive spirit in their children will make them lose in today's world. But they do not realize that it takes a heavy toll on the mental and physical health of their children. Children should be encouraged and induced to study more and more and perform up to their best capability but it need not be in comparison with some other children. Each child should be trained by the parents and teachers to do his or her best unconcerned about the level of performance of the other children by strengthening their own talents, skills and capabilities. The children should not be pressurized to achieve everything what all the other children are achieving. This will only weaken them physically and mentally and will make them lose their physical health and become stressful, tense, anxious and so on due to the pressure and stress that they are unable to withstand. Most of the children in today's world are overburdened with the level of competition that they have to face in life so that they become the most successful in their group. This results in many negative tendencies in them like anxiety, stress, extreme competitiveness, jealousy and so on. No doubt they may become the most successful- but at what cost? One may become materially successful in the world but he will turn out to be one who is full of negative tendencies because he grew with much negativity in him. We must understand that man does not live for worldly success alone. There are so many important human values to which he must pay his attention to".

"There are also parents who scold their children with harsh words and give them physical punishment that make their children feel insulted and consequently their ego gets hurt. Some parents also resort to these measures when they find anything wrong with their children. But then such parents first of all should become aware of their own defects and they must understand that their children act in a particular incorrect manner because the parents themselves have passed on their own defects to their children. Many a time parents also compare their children with other children who have fared better in the class. But such comparisons are unnecessary. But even if such comparisons are made it should be such that it helps and induces their children to perform better. Whenever the teachers compare a bright student's performance and success with that of a poor student's performance, they should bear in mind that such comparisons do not belittle the child. They should avoid stressing his inabilities as this will make the child feel disheartened and depressed and also lose his self-esteem and confidence level. Parents also make such comparisons. Actually it is the love and affection for their children that make the parents act like this. They are afraid that if they are not strict with their children, scold them and punish them for not performing well, or for not listening to their words or for not behaving as per their wish then their children will lose in future.

But it is only through love that both parents and teachers can bring about the desired changes and improvements in children. Harsh words and punishments will only create negative tendencies like hatred, anger, discontentment, inferiority complex, diffidence, and stress and so on in children. First and foremost the parents and teachers should try to become the role models for children so that they set an example for all that they desire and expect from children.

Our scriptures mention four gradual steps in this regard. They are *Sama* or good words, *Dana* that means giving some concessions, *Bheda* that is threatening and finally *Dhanda* or punishment. So I wish the parents and teachers try to follow these four steps one after the other as per their order so that they can bring about the desired improvements in their children. Parents and teachers should also try to inculcate moral and ethical values and principles in children as these are certainly far more important than worldly material success".

"*Abraham Lincoln* once wrote a letter to his son's Headmaster of the school where his son was studying. He wrote,"

"Respected Teacher,

My son will have to learn I know that all men are not just, all men are not true. But teach him also that for every scoundrel there is a hero; that for every selfish politician, there is a dedicated leader. Teach him that for every enemy there is a friend. It will take time, I know; but teach him, if you can, that a dollar earned is far more valuable than five found. Teach him to learn to lose and also to enjoy winning. Steer him away from envy, if you can. Teach him the secret of quite laughter. Let him learn early that the bullies are the easiest to tick. Teach him, if you can, the wonder of books; but also give him quiet time to ponder over the eternal mystery of birds in the sky, bees in the sun, and flowers on a green hill–side.

In school teach him it is far more honorable to fail than to cheat. Teach him to have faith in his own ideas, even if everyone tells him they are wrong. Teach him to be gentle with gentle people and tough with the tough. Try to give my son the strength not to follow the crowd when everyone is getting on the bandwagon.

Teach him to listen to all men but teach him also to filter all he hears on a screen of truth and take only the good that comes through. Teach him, if you can how to laugh when he is sad. Teach him there is no shame in tears. Teach him to scoff at cynics and to beware of too much sweetness. Teach him to sell his brawn and brain to the highest bidders; but never to put a price tag on his heart and soul. Teach him to close his ears to a howling mob... and to stand and fight if he thinks he's right. Treat him gently; but do not cuddle him because only the test of fire makes fine steel. Let him have the courage to be impatient, let him have the patience to be brave. Teach him always to have sublime faith in himself because then he will always have sublime faith in mankind. This is a big order; but see what you can do. He is such a fine little fellow, my son."

"We should make children understand that we, as human beings should give more importance to human values. Competition is conspicuous even in the animal kingdom. That comes under the basic nature of any being. But values are relevant and are meant only for humans, the highest species on earth. So it is only proper that man gives more importance to these values. Children must be made to understand that only those who possess positive values can become happy and peaceful always in their life and this is what each and every human being craves for and the virtues or positive values one will be able to follow only when one can increase his positivity and reduce his negativity with positivity".

"From what you said I understand that we should never fail to recognize and encourage the positive qualities that we see in children so that we can empower them more and more and similarly we should also detect the negative qualities in children and help them to get over them in a very friendly and understanding way. Now suddenly I remember something about my own behavior though cannot be categorized as negative but was definitely not good that my mother could eliminate from me through her understanding of my psychology. It happened when I was barely three years old it seems. I came to know about that through my mother as I was very small then. Will you please permit me to say that to you Swamiji"?

"Definitely; go ahead. Tell me so that I too can listen to you" said the *Swamiji*.

"It seems once after coming back from our native village in Kerala where we went to spend a few days, I got the habit of tearing to pieces all the cloth in the house whether it was towels or the *Dhothis* of my father or the *Sarees* of my mother and so on. When my mother detected that I continued with my behavior in spite of her telling me repeatedly not to do such a thing she got annoyed with me and scolded me for that. When I started crying she took pity on me and leaving all her work she came to me and pacified me and told me softly that I should not repeat that act again. As usual I told her that I will not repeat it any more. Then it seems my mother began to think why I did like that and what made me tear all the clothes into small pieces that looked like ribbons. Then she suddenly remembered the person in our native place who used to visit all the houses in the village asking for food. As he was a poor person without any one whom he can call his own and as he was slightly mentally imbalanced person though good, everyone took pity on him and wherever he went they gave him food. It was a regular thing in the village. Though he was a harmless person, the strange thing about him was that whenever anyone gave him towels or *Dhothis* he wore them only after tearing them in to long thin pieces. It seems this thought came to my mother's mind suddenly and she understood that it was because I saw him in the village I took a fancy to tear into pieces any cloth that I saw and then it seems after she completed her cooking she called me to her side and after cajoling me asked me in a very loving and understanding way why I am tearing the clothes in the house like that. It seems I told her that somehow I feel like tearing the clothes when I see them. Then it seems she asked me to tell her whenever I got the urge of tearing anything and without my knowledge she took all the old useless torn *Dhothis*, towels and *Sarees* that she could find in the house and every time when I told her that I wanted to tear the clothes she put before me the old clothes and asked me to tear them until I got satisfied and this went on a few times and very soon I got over that habit and that urge in me. Now I understand how important it is to know the psychology of children so that we can show them the right path."

"Now I would like to ask you Swamiji, Can one who tries to improve himself by trying to generate positivity and wipe out his negativity by positivity expect to get the best possible life With peace and happiness quickly"?

"Self-improvement is a process. It is a journey. All on a sudden no one will be able to become completely positive without any trace of negativity. It will take time. Any change for better takes time normally. This is because one's nature is shaped by his past tendencies and several other factors since his birth. As his efforts so will be the result. It is also not possible to fix any time limit for reaching the desired goal. It is the journey that is important. Normally when you start the journey then automatically you are bound to reach the destination. There is no need for you to know how far you have come or how much distance you have covered or how long the journey will take or how soon you will reach the destination and so on. It is unnecessary and it will also divert your attention from your efforts.

Every step in your journey will take you nearer and nearer to your goal automatically. When a student without concentrating on the lessons that he is learning goes on turning the pages of the book to see how many pages of the book he has covered or how many pages are more for him to cover, can never reach the goal soon as his attention is diverted from actual study. So it is better that one forgets about the time factor in reaching the goal. For some the journey may be shorter while for some others it may be longer although the destination is the same for all. It all depends upon the fact when you start your journey and from where, that is, at what point you start your journey. For the one who is already virtuous the journey to reach the destination will take only less time as he is like one who has not started his journey from the starting point but from somewhere in the middle because he had covered some part of his journey already in his present or in his past births. This does not however mean that one should postpone starting his journey towards the best possible life."

"Does duality really exist, Swamiji?"

"In the case of great souls whom we call as saints and for whom there is equanimity of vision neither good nor bad affects them and this makes them go beyond both good as well as bad. For such souls, duality does not exist because they know that all dualities of life, all differentiations into bad and good, positive and negative are the result of our own perceptions and are there because we compare one with the other. Bad exists because we perceive the good and we see the good because we perceive something as bad in this world. It is our perception that makes something as bad or good because many a time what is good for some at any point of time may turn out to be bad for the others or at some other moments for the same person. If either positivity or negativity alone exists then where is the distinction? That means all these distinctions are manmade, that is inside man, the created being. Anything that brings about unhappiness or is harmful to one and the others we call it bad or negative and anything that results in good or happiness to oneself and the others we call it positive or good.

The world, the very creation is a mixture of good and bad, pleasant and unpleasant and so on for normal ordinary humans. But when one becomes totally pure, in all his thoughts, emotions, feelings, words and actions then he goes beyond the distinction of either bad or good that means he goes beyond all dualities of life because nothing is either good or bad for him. He is indifferent to the dualities of life because he becomes a personification of all that is pure. To such a pure mind everything in this world is pure and what all he sees, hears, tastes, smells, touches and experiences is nothing but pure and he views all dualities of life as the same. When that is the case where is the bad or negative for him? All his thoughts, words and deeds become positive. He thinks, speaks and acts only good not because that will bring him reward later but because he feels that it is his duty to think, speak and act in a virtuous manner. It becomes his very nature to do good and good alone always without the least conscious effort because he becomes a personification of all that is pure and for such a person, who is an elevated soul with a pure mind there is no such distinction into good or bad because to him everything is pure. The sage who goes beyond worldly life becomes fully aware of this fact, the reality, that these dualities only belong to worldly men. An average man either becomes happy and peaceful or unhappy and miserable because of these dualities".

"The great *Mahatmas* or great souls have not only understood but experienced that in reality it is our perception or understanding of a certain information that is based upon our past lives experiences some of which we are aware of and some of which lay buried deep inside our memory in the sub conscious mind without our own knowing at our conscious level, and our conditioning or belief that form the thoughts in our mind that make us to see and experience the dualities in life. Our thoughts based upon our perception get categorized in to good or bad and they become feelings, attitude or emotions in our mind and they are expressed in words and deeds. Good thoughts lead to positivity and bad thoughts result in negativity in man. We perceive anything as good because we think that it will make us happy, cheerful, and peaceful and so on and people welcome it. We perceive anything as bad because we think that it will result in bad, that means, unhappiness, misery and so on which people want to avoid. The great souls are also aware that perceptions can influence only one's physical body and mind but not one's soul and that in reality we are neither the body nor mind but the pure soul that does not see or experience or gets affected by any of the duality seen in the world".

How to achieve the best possible life"?

"Since an average worldly person, because of his limitations is unable to reach the ideal state of best life, the best alternative for him is the best possible life that will ensure and guarantee considerable happiness and peace for him and for all the others who come in to contact with him."

"For achieving peace and happiness through best possible life every one of us should make a conscious effort to understand our mind in an impartial manner as a witness, know our strengths and weaknesses, the good as well as the bad in us that means all that are positive and all that are negative in us- our virtues and vices, and then reduce the bad, the negative, the vices and enhance the good, the positive that are the virtues. It is up to us to ignore and pluck out the weeds of negativity or bad in us as far as possible and fill the place with good and positive because only positivity or goodness in one will make one always happy and peaceful while what we consider or perceive as bad or negative in any one will create nothing but unhappiness, misery and lack of peace for oneself and for the others. The tales in the ancient scriptures relating to the killing of the demons by the gods is symbolic of the annihilation of the negativity inside us with our positivity".

"We have to seek answers from within ourselves. No doubt it is very essential that one should know how to make a living but more importantly one should know how to live and lead a life of fulfillment, happiness and peace. Since all our thoughts, words and deeds are aimed at achieving happiness and peace we should always try our best to be positive.

Sometimes we project our negativity because we, in an ignorant manner believe that it will make us happy. This ignorance must be removed through proper knowledge and awareness so that man after realizing the fact that negativity wherever and in whichever manner is present will only make one unhappy and sad and with negativity in him one cannot bring forth his best in his life.

One should plant the idea of the best possible life for him through repeated thinking because thought is the root from which both positivity as well as negativity appear and come out through words and deeds. It is also a fact that any single positive emotion is bound to create a series of positive feelings and any negative emotion will generate a series of negative feelings in man. For example when we are sympathetic towards another's pain or misery or suffering then it creates a feeling of love, and kindness in us. These gradually become empathy that culminates in compassion that is one of the highest virtues of life. Similarly the feeling of jealousy in one will automatically trigger the feeling of hatred and then anger towards the other person. So if we are able to create at least one single thought of positivity then many other virtues will follow that automatically. So also if we are able to banish from our heart one single negative feeling then it can help us in removing many other negative feelings from us without effort. That is because whatever emotions or thoughts we have that one will become more and deep rooted in our mind. Positive thoughts in our mind will generate more and more positive feelings leading to positive words and actions. Similarly, if we want to eliminate any negative thought then that will induce the elimination of more and more of such thoughts and feelings or emotions, words and deeds.

Negativity by spreading negative energy will pollute everyone and everything and also the atmosphere around us whereas positive energy will purify not only the sender and the receiver of such energy but it will also purify the entire atmosphere. But then a single foot step cannot make a path. We have to walk again and again for making a path. Similarly, a single good or positive thought that is a passing one and that does not make a deep impression in us cannot create or make a habit in us to think all that is good in a natural manner. We have to make a deep mental path by thinking all that are positive and virtuous and their good effects over and over again in a repeated manner so that such thoughts arise in the mind in a casual, automatic, and natural manner, so that thinking positively can become our very nature. Once we start generating more and more positivity in us by following as many virtues as possible then in course of time without any effort one will be able to project Positivity all the time because it will become his habit and his very nature to think, speak and act positively. As *Gautam Buddha* has said, what you think you become. If one repeatedly thinks all that are positive then it is bound to grow multifold and the mind will find its own ways to achieve the goal of the best possible in life.

We must make a vow and determine to make our life the best possible one that is purposeful and worthy for ourselves as well as for the others and whatever may be the challenges and setbacks in our efforts we should have the necessary courage and determination so that all the failures or setbacks do not dishearten us and make us stop our efforts to reach the goal that we have set. We should work continuously to achieve the goal of life even if are not rewarded up to our satisfaction because sincere and honest efforts for the wellbeing of oneself and that of others will never go unrewarded; if not immediately at least in the long run, if not now at least later, if not in this birth at least in some future birth one is bound to reap the reward".

"In order to reach the desired objective of peace and happiness in life first of all we should examine our nature and tendencies with an open mind in an impartial, unbiased manner and try to know our weaknesses that are the negative tendencies and our positive tendencies. Many a time we are biased and try to justify our own negative emotions and behavior and also blame the others and situations and circumstances for our own weaknesses and for our own negativity. But such biased analysis will only hinder and block us from improving ourselves. We must be honest enough to admit our mistakes at least in our mind and resolve not to repeat such things again. Open admission of one's own mistakes is definitely magnanimous. However only one who is royal, magnanimous and with a brave heart can admit his weaknesses openly. We must at least be honest to ourselves in admitting our mistakes and accepting our negativities within ourselves if not openly.

Many a time in order to give a good impression of ourselves to others we try to cover up our weaknesses. But the fact is though one can cheat the others he cannot cheat his own self. The inner voice will always prick him for all his negative thoughts and bad attitudes and behavior. It is also a fact that one cannot cheat the others all the time. Sooner or later people will come to know of one's real nature.

We must also try our best to see the positive side in other's negativity and try to view things objectively. That means, we must be capable of understanding the other's point of view as well. We must also review our thoughts, behavior, words and acts at each step, if not all the time, at least once a day preferably when we go to bed in the night. Our mind should be made into a diary wherein we record at the end of each day preferably just before going to bed in the night, all our positive and negative emotions, feelings, thoughts and the negative and the positive words we uttered and all our actions on that day. We should resolve to continue and if possible make an improvement of all the positive feelings, words and actions that had happened that day. All the negative thoughts and emotions, words uttered and actions performed on that day must be pondered over and analyzed. One should then make a resolve to plant positive emotions in the place of the negative ones.

Mere setting up of a goal or objective will not serve any purpose unless one actually puts in the required effort for achieving the desired goal. Mere desire for improving oneself will not take oneself anywhere near the goal of life. So after analyzing and understanding his negativity one should try to fill his mind with positive qualities so that he can remove his negative tendencies. After this one should immediately start practising positive qualities without any delay. As he practices positivity, he should also analyze as to how much he is able to fill his mind with positivity and what are the problems he is facing in practicing positivity and how to overcome the obstacles and so on. If one does not do these then mere knowing of his negativity will never take him anywhere near his goal of Peace and Happiness as his knowledge about his negativity will be only theoretical without any benefit to anyone".

"If we examine ourselves honestly then we will come to know that almost all our thoughts are about the outside world and ourselves in relation to the world, with its varied objects, people and situations and so on. Barely we turn our attention and thoughts inward to examine our own mind and its nature, the positive and negative thoughts that arise in our mind that lead to corresponding words and deeds and their results, what qualities we have to empower ourselves with and which are the qualities that we have to destroy, what is our real objective in life, how are we to attain that and what are we doing to reach our goal and so on. If only we can set apart some time for knowing the answers for all these and mold our life in such a way that we become the best possible human beings then it is a great art that will culminate in peace and happiness for all in this world".

"There are people who lecture and give discourses on positivity without following them in their own life. Such people also can never reach the goal of the best possible life. Merely preaching about the positive qualities may give one some satisfaction but it can't transform one's mind or that of others. So, mere theoretical knowledge about one's negativity will be of no use to anyone. Those who listen to such people also will not get any benefit out of this because they will not follow their preaching as they themselves fail to practice what they preach.. So such theoretical knowledge will benefit none."

"One need not brood over one's past negativity, instead one should try to learn from his past mistakes and make a resolve not only not to repeat them again but also replace them with positive emotions, words and actions. We have to think of the past in a way that we visit them but we should not stay there permanently because if we do so then we will get stuck without making any progress. The past should be reviewed in an impartial manner and what all are to be discarded must be removed and what are all to be entertained and strengthened must be strengthened. To that extent only the past must be brought in to the picture. Repentance for all the negativities of the past that are bad thoughts, words and deeds should help a person to prevent repeating the mistakes of the past due to his past negativity, by generating positivity. But if one merely repents for his bad behavior of the past at a certain emotional moment and forgets about it later, and if he continues to behave in the same old manner without realizing his mistakes then repentance will serve no purpose at all. But once the purpose that is avoiding negativity as a result of repentance for his negativity of the past is served then, the past must be forgotten totally. Remembering the past permanently is of no use but a great burden that need not be carried throughout our life time because not only that it will not serve any purpose but it will also make us either guilty or egoistic depending upon whether we exhibited negativity or positivity then, in the past".

"The next step is to make a vow to do all that we can to enhance our positivity and minimize our negativity. We have to start each day with a thankful heart for all the blessings of life and with a determination that we will create happiness and thereby peace not only for ourselves but for all those around us by our thoughts, words and deeds. We should become more and more positive and less and less negative each day. Every morning as soon as we get up we must make a determination that we will be a better person that day than the previous day and we should also convert this determination in to action.

Spending some time alone quietly also gives us an opportunity to examine ourselves openly and honestly because it makes our mind calm, and the overcrowding of thoughts that pass through our mind also will get reduced and the mind will become quieter and quieter as time passes. When the thoughts get reduced to the minimum possible then our own consciousness, our innermost voice that is the witness will make us know the truth. Self-introspection and self-analysis or self-enquiry is not possible in a mind that is perturbed and overcrowded with thoughts.

Many a time we are able to detect our mistakes or negativities and if only we are sensitive enough and good enough then we are sure to admit our mistakes at least silently though not openly and refrain ourselves from committing such mistakes in the form of vices again. But in many cases people do not spend enough time for self-analysis and introspection and even if they spend some time and remember their mistakes they try to justify themselves and continue to behave in the same old manner. But for such a person the best possible life is a very remote possibility. It only shows his mental contamination levels. Such people are a gone case. Nothing can be done about them. Perhaps they may learn the hard way, when they face the most adverse situations in their life because adversities, setbacks and failures make a man humble enough to admit and rectify all his mistakes".

"In our journey of self-improvement, we should also never bother about others in the sense, whether they recognize our positive behavior, whether they reciprocate our positivity towards them and whether they also try to project and radiate positivity. We must go on in our determined efforts to fill ourselves with positivity. When we practice this every day and if possible throughout the day then the peace and happiness that we experience at the end of the day is bound to be tremendous and the next day we are bound to wake up fresh, energetic and with more positivity than the previous day. We should also notice our negative tendencies, words and deeds that we have within ourselves and also that we project and try to reduce them as much as we can. We should make a vow as to not to repeat them. This will also make us lovable to others resulting in more happiness and peace to ourselves and for the others.

We know from our experience that even a single positive feeling, or emotion, word or deed from us results in immense satisfaction and happiness and peace to ourselves and to the others. When that is the case then how much joy and peace one will be able to experience when he fills his mind and project as much positivity as is possible for him? We should never give up this regular exercise".

"Mind easily gets attracted towards negativity because negative qualities are easier to follow and it also gives a sense of triumph in one by boosting one's ego and they also make one to forget his problems and difficulties and they appear to be giving happiness temporarily. This is also because we think wrongly that they give us happiness. But one must clearly understand that all negativity will ultimately lead to misery, sorrow, unhappiness and lack of peace in one's life. On the other hand positive qualities or the virtues are very difficult to follow. One will have to face many hurdles and setbacks in worldly life if one adheres to the *Dharmic* path or the path of virtues. But one must realize that if one goes on practicing positive qualities in spite of all the setbacks, difficulties and impediments that he has to face in his life on account of that, then the treasure house of everlasting peace and happiness will be waiting for him sooner or later. This fact one should never forget in his life time. If he remembers this truth always then he will always turn his body and mind far away from all that are negative and will instead adhere and will stick to the path of virtues or positivity only".

"The entire cosmos is permeated by energy, so also the beings in the universe. Within each being there is constant exchange of energies into positive or negative. Thoughts are the energies that influence the wellbeing of body, mind and spirit. Our physical body is influenced by both by external factors as well as by thoughts and emotions. It is our thoughts and our emotions that mold our behavior. Positive or constructive thoughts or positivity generate positive energy in us. They flow out and also return to us in the same or in greater measure. So also is the case with negativity or negative qualities, thoughts and emotions that are ruinous and destructive".

"Strangely enough when we are able to strengthen one positive quality in us then all the other virtues will get into us without much effort. Similar is the case with negativity too. If we are careless in detecting and getting over a single negativity in us then even without our knowledge more and more negativity will creep into our mind. This realization and the effort in filling one's mind with positivity in the journey of one's life will make one's life purposeful and worthy and it will result in happiness and peace not only for oneself but for all the others around him and finally when the time to depart from the world comes that one will leave this world with a sense of total fulfillment because he did justice to his birth as a human being by doing his best in his life and also for the others by being the best that he is capable of by living his life with maximum possibility".

"We should not bother about others thoughts, words or actions towards us. It is up to them to entertain any types of feelings or thoughts- negative or positive. We need not get influenced or overpowered by other's criticisms about us, their comments, their thoughts, words or actions. We have no right to change others. It is also not possible. Do not complain about the thorns in the rose plant that hurt you but rejoice because the plant has lovely roses too. Enjoy its smoothness and fragrance and forget about the thorns. After all thorns too serve some purpose, maybe they are there to protect the delicate roses. Who knows? So to achieve happiness and peace in our life we must bring the necessary changes in our mind. That only is possible. If everyone at least most of us can do that then the whole world will become a heaven on earth".

"In such a cleaning process it is possible that in the beginning more and more negative tendencies may crop up in the mind because all our submerged negative tendencies may surface. It is like cleaning a floor that has a lot of accumulated, layers and layers of dust and dirt. As and when we wash the room all the accumulated dirt that had set in strongly on the floor may come up and it may become very difficult to wash and clean the floor perfectly. The more we wash the more will be the dirt that will come up on the surface from the bottom. But without giving up if we continue to pour more and more water and wash the floor then it is bound to become very clean since all the accumulated dirt and dust are bound to get washed off at least gradually after a continuous washing of the floor. The Hindu *Puranic* story of churning of the ocean of milk by the *Devas*, the Gods on one side and *Asuras* or the demons on the other side and the emergence of all that are poisonous and bad in the beginning stages of churning and the emergence of nectar or *Amrutha* in the end clearly reveals this fact.

We humans are a mixture of both –good as well as bad. But then we know that our goal is to become good or the divine but not to be bad or demonic. So we churn our mind through sincere, honest introspection. In this process all the dirt, all the accumulated negative tendencies are bound to come up on the surface. But unmindful of that and without yielding ourselves to those negative tendencies if we continue to ponder over all the good and bad within us, and become good and positive by all means, then finally the nectar, the happiness and peace that is the outcome of all our virtues will come up on its own accord and this will give us everlasting peace and happiness that is termed as Bliss.

Cleaning our mind no doubt is a difficult task. All our accumulated tendencies of the past will come up on the surface of our mind making our mind more and more impure. Our mind will also find new arguments and ways to justify our negative emotions. For example one may start thinking what is the use of being good to others? Who knows for certain whether one can achieve the set goal at all? Even if there is certainty about the result, how long to continue with such efforts? How long to wait patiently? And so on. But with persistent and continuous efforts one will be able to realize the goal at least gradually. One need not get disheartened or disappointed if he does not make any progress in the beginning stages of one's determined efforts. Without bothering about the outcome we should go on continuously with our efforts. We should have the determination that we will never turn back or stop our efforts whatever may be the hurdles, disappointments or setbacks in our efforts. Reaching the objective may not be immediate or now but it is not never. Every effort is bound to generate a particular result- good will generate good bad will generate bad. As it is said, the only time that we fail in our life is when we fall down and decide to stay there."

"In one's effort to improve oneself one should also not allow himself to degrade himself when he realizes all his negativity as a result of his honest introspection of himself. There is no need for us to be judgmental. We need not judge and pass judgment on ourselves and categorize us as either bad or good. It is also not proper or possible to judge others. With self-analysis we should only try to know our weaknesses or negative qualities or the virtues and merits in us and then generate and strengthen our virtues on the one hand and eradicate the negativity or vices in us with our virtues that can be termed as positive qualities.

After all life is not a straight line but a wavy one. There are bound to be ups and downs, happiness and miseries, bad as well as good in all. We need not ruin our happiness just by detecting our negative behavior. One should not become guilty or diffident when one comes to know of his negative emotions. We have to understand that these are all part of our life. Without attaching undue importance to it we should try not to repeat such tendencies in future. There is no need to hold on to our past, already over negative behavior. It is of no use. It will only harm us in lowering our self-esteem and it will also put hurdles in our path towards self-improvement. Also we should not be elated or become proud of ourselves whenever we identify the positivity in us. We should only try to enhance our positivity. We have to just concentrate on today not on our entire life period because it is neither possible nor necessary."

"No doubt to fill one's mind with positivity and remove negativity thereby is a very difficult task. But greatest things can be done in this world only by great sacrifices. It is also a fact that nothing worthwhile can be accomplished without obstructions and failures. It is only those who persevere till the end that succeed and reach the goal. When you seek the highest, aim at the highest then you shall reach the highest sooner or later. This is the cosmic law. Rome was not built in a day. Whenever you face failures or hurdles in your endeavor towards the best possible life, then do not bother about individual happenings but unmindful of such things go on with perseverance, courage and faith in reaching your goal. In this journey of yours do not look at the waves, the individual happenings, incidents and your sacrifices but look at the vast ocean, the totality and your destination. The waves may come up and disappear after some time. They are all temporary. The end that is the ultimate, the ocean is what is important. Bear that in mind and act".

"Material success and happiness may be obtained by working harder, smarter and with sincere, continuous efforts. But although material success is a necessary factor in one's life, it is not everything. One should also not hanker after material success and prosperity too much because in the long run this may create many vices and many negative tendencies in one. The more we achieve the more we crave for and the more we achieve the more will be our tension and anxiety to protect and safeguard our material wealth and in the process of achieving more and safeguarding what one has achieved, more and more negative tendencies may come up and may grow in our mind. That means too much craving for material prosperity will damage our happiness and peace. On the other hand, all efforts to enhance and fill ourselves with positivity and gradually eliminate the negative tendencies in us thereby will enlarge our mind and it will create happiness and peace for ourselves and also for the others and this will make our life worthy and purposeful. If everyone tries to change himself for good, to become positive in his thoughts, feelings, words and deeds then the whole world will become good and there will be only positivity everywhere and anywhere.

After all it is not the length of life that counts but its performance. It is not how long we lived that matters but how we lived that counts because we are not here merely to make a living. We are here to enrich ourselves and the world at the same time by our life because our life is a divine gift and it is only proper that we give back our life to the divine with this offering of what we did with our life and how we made our life the best that was possible for us".

"Swamiji tell me something about the human energy field and how it affects us"?

"The human energy field or the aura is invisible and it surrounds all around our body for about four to five feet in the case of people with an average health. It is the halo surrounding our body. It is an electromagnetic field that surrounds, penetrates and extends beyond our physical body. This aura represents our physical, mental and spiritual energies of a person. It is found to be depleted in the case of unhealthy persons. Everything in this universe is energy and the aura surrounds both animate beings as well as inanimate things like rocks etc. Matter that appears to be solid is actually made up of energy that vibrates at specific frequency that gives matter shape, size, and texture and so on. Even the cells in our body are actually made up of vibratory energy particles. When these particles vibrate a small electrical impulse is generated in our body and when there is an electrical field around our body a magnetic field gets developed automatically. These tiny electrical impulses in our body result in the formation of magnetic field around our body that is known as aura. Positivity helps in expanding our aura whereas negativity contracts our aura".

"One should understand that the negative emotions in us block the energy field of our body. When we create positive feelings or emotions these blockages are removed and the energy flows without any hindrance.

An energy field or aura that is the electromagnetic field surrounding an object can either emit or absorb. So when we entertain negative thoughts in us or from other people then negative energy builds up in our system and it emits negative vibrations from us or absorbs negative vibrations from the others and damages both the sender as well as the recipient of that energy. In contrast to this when one receives positive energy or sends positive energy then positive vibrations are received or sent out and this results in enhancing the mental well-being of the person resulting in happiness and peace for both the sender as well as the receiver. So it is highly necessary that while we enhance the positive tendencies in us to the maximum, we must also reduce the negative tendencies to the minimum level as much as possible so that we lead the best possible life on earth.

We must understand that the negative qualities or vices in us create more and more negative feelings in us that result in depletion of positive energy in us that cause an overall ill health.

On the other hand, generation of more and more positivity in us will increase our positive energy resulting in physical, mental and spiritual health. This is because more and more positivity will result in more and more positive energy in one and less and less positivity or more and more negativity will lead to more and more negative energy in one resulting in depletion of all the energy in one. As our ultimate aim is to increase positive energy and decrease negative energy we should try to imbibe as many virtues as possible in our life. What we want in the end is a healthy body with a healthy mind and a healthy mind in a healthy body".

"Swamiji, you said that it is our perception that is responsible for the good and bad in this world. But how does it happen? Kindly explain this to me".

"Yes. As I have already said, it is our perception of objects, persons, situations and events in the world that create good or positive, bad or negative impressions in our mind and these create negative or positive thoughts, feelings or emotions that are expressed through words and actions. Perception that is only cognition or understanding takes place in the mind where thoughts are generated. The sensory organs are only the windows that send the information of sight, taste, smell, or hearing or the sensation of touch into the mind in which the brain or the faculty of understanding and discrimination is a part. It is here the differentiation or categorization of any of the information sent by the senses takes place as per the perception or understanding. If certain information is characterized as negative then the corresponding negative thought arises in the mind and vice versa."

"If we are able to perceive everything positively then there will not be any negativity in us or outside us. But then such a state of perception is possible only for advanced and elevated beings. They perceive everything outside them in an impartial manner like a witness or as a mere observer. To them there is no categorization of information in to bad or negative or good or positive. But we the ordinary worldly human beings categorize everything into good and bad because we take or perceive them either as good or bad depending upon whether they are favorable to us or not. When they are favorable to us we call it good and bad when they are unfavorable to us and these perceptions of ours create positive or negative thought in us with good or bad, positive or negative consequences. Once we are able to realize this fundamental truth then we will be able to bring about the necessary changes in us for good. But many a time we know this fact only in a theoretical manner but we become helpless in establishing that thought in us. This is because of our desires, attachments, expectations and the most important, the ego in us. Once we are able to reduce these limitations in us then it will become easy for us to remove negativity and inculcate positivity in us- and that will make all the difference in our lives."

"*Aurobindo* in his 'In living within' says, "If you look at yourself carefully, you will realize the one carries in oneself the opposites. Within you there is the light and shadow. For example, if you observe yourself you will find that at one moment you are very generous, broadminded, kind etc. At another moment the opposite- you are jealous, envious, narrow minded etc. One does not pay attention to this and that is why all these things live comfortably together as neighbors. One must first discover them and prevent them from intermingling in one's consciousness. Separate the shadow from the light; later you can get rid of the shadow".

"Can negative thoughts, feelings and acts be compensated with those of positivity Swamiji"?

"Very many times we try to compensate the effects of any of our negativity with positivity. Suppose somebody was rude to someone else or cheated him and caused mental agony to him. Later when he happens to regret for his negative actions then he tries to compensate his negative action of the past by being very kind to some other person or by making some charity. By such an act he feels that he can compensate for his negative action. But then it is not so. Each one will have to shoulder the responsibility for each of his thoughts, words and acts. One will have to suffer the consequence of his negativity however small it may be. He cannot undo the effects of either of his positivity or negativity, as each account is separate.

Man has both positivity as well as negativity in him. So automatically he will reap the effects of positivity and will have to bear the results of his negativity separately. When you sow the seed of a poisonous plant only the poisonous seedling will sprout from the seed. However much you want an apple tree from that it can't just happen. Any amount of positive behavior cannot cancel the effects of one's negativity however small it may be. That means one should always be careful and be aware of his thoughts, words and deeds and generate only positivity at the same time remove our negative thoughts so that only positive effect will come. What we sow only we can reap".

"What should one do for improving oneself"?

"In order to improve ourselves we should decide to imbibe positivity and eliminate negativity in us. For this one should see, hear and speak all that are positive and avoid seeing, hearing and speaking all that are negative. One may also follow any religious, spiritual or scientific or any other methods to generate positive thoughts to form the positive tendencies in one that come out in the form of positive words and actions. Prayer, practicing yoga and meditation, listening to spiritual discourses, reading, understanding and following the moral and ethical codes mentioned in the scriptures, *Satsang* or being in good company etc. are meant only to make man pure and divine with all positive values of life.

If our intellect is filled with good information in the morning when we are fresh then its effect will continue for the whole day. So also negative information that we gather in the morning will lead to negative thoughts and this will enhance the negativity in one for the whole day. This is because in the morning when we are fresh and clear in our mind it is easy for any thought to settle in the memory and make an impression there deeply. If we gather unnecessary information that are useless for us then such information will create unnecessary wasteful thoughts in our mind that will deplete our energy and we become mentally weak to that extent. So as far as possible we should try to gather positive information that are positive and useful during the morning time so that it will make us good human beings full of positive energy the whole day. If we practice this everyday then without much effort we can become positive and good always.

Whenever any unnecessary or negative information reach us then immediately we have to brush it aside without allowing such information to settle in our memory so that we do not allow our energy either to get depleted or wasted or turn negative with negative consequences. For this one should make use of the discriminatory powers of his intellect to gather information that are only useful and good and that enhance the positivity".

"What is body-mind-spirit harmony? How does this harmony promote the best possible life for one"?

"In making one's life the most beneficial and useful to one self as well as for the others one should also bear in mind that one's effort in enhancing positive qualities or virtues in one's mind has a great bearing on his physical health. So also the one who is enjoying a good physical health will be able to become aware of the virtues and practice them without much difficulty because his sound physical health helps and contributes significantly in making his mind happy and peaceful and healthy by having and projecting all that we call as positive. For example a person who has a poor health or suffering from any physical problem and is suffering from some physical disease or pain due to injury, or due to old age etc. cannot be cheerful, and healthy mentally because his physical condition makes him sad, helpless, discontented, complaining, full of self-pity, pessimistic, diffident, dependent, unhappy and so on and he will fail to perceive anything positive either in himself or in others or in situations. So, one should try his level best to be physically hale and healthy, so that, his poor health or ill health does not become a cause for his mental illness that shows itself through his negativity. For this one must first of all take proper nourishing food at proper intervals. One should also avoid food that damages the body and mind as well as the spirit, even if they are tasty. Sufficient and good sleep and physical exercises are the other contributing factors for a good physical well-being. Last but not the least one must also build up good habits like getting up early in the morning, taking early morning bath, walking straight, avoiding sleep during the day time and so on.

The ancient Indian Rishis pointed out that the physical body is made up of seven *Dhatus* or constitutional elements, namely *Rasa* or fluid, *Raktha* or blood, *Mamsa* or muscle, *Majja* or marrow, *Asthi* or bone, *Meda* or brain and spinal cord, and *Sukla* or *Ojas* or sperm and physical health strengthens these.

If one is able to be positive in his tendencies and behavior in spite of physical ill health, pain and suffering then it is a great achievement because it shows how strong and healthy his mind is. Similarly, the one who is full of negativity is unlikely to be physically fit and healthy. This is because physical and mental wellbeing are closely related to each other. However the one who is mentally very strong and healthy will not get disheartened and become negative in his outlook and behavior even if he is suffering any amount of physical pain whatever may the reasons. This is because the more subtle a thing is more is its power. The physical body is gross whereas the mind is less gross than the physical body and it is also subtle as well. That is why the physical body is called matter and the mind is called the subtle matter. In ancient Indian spirituality mind is called as the subtle body or *Sukshma Sareera* in Sanskrit language. It is also more powerful than the physical body.

Further, while the physical health mainly depends upon various external factors that are beyond our control, our mental health solely depends upon factors that can be brought under one's own control in spite of the fact that mind has accumulated tendencies of several births. The desired changes can be brought about in these tendencies that are inside one with a strong will power. If the inherent tendency of a person is negative then that can be arrested to a large extent by deliberately, willingly creating positive tendencies and attitudes. This is possible because man is endowed with intelligence that can discriminate good from bad. He is also endowed with a will of his own and he is given the freedom to choose".

"Apart from this, the physical and mental health also in turn influence the spiritual well-being of a person. If one is mentally and physically ill then it affects the spiritual well- being of that individual because only in a sound body that contains a sound mind any spiritual progress that culminates in total awareness of 'who we are' becomes a possibility by knowing, transforming and transcending one's mind. By knowing one's mind, its attitudes and tendencies one understands his defects as well as merits and by transforming his mind he is in a position to eliminate all negative thoughts and tendencies and enhance all that are positive. When a person is able to reach this stage he becomes mentally very healthy and pure and then it is not very difficult for him to transcend the mind and attain spiritual wellbeing. Such a person will become an embodiment of all virtues with no vices and this gives him permanent peace and happiness that is termed as Bliss or *Ananda.* But actually, for a person who is spiritually elevated having a good or poor physical health is immaterial because to him the gross body with all its sensory and the other organs is meant only to carry on the biological and physiological functions . But if one has a poor mental well-being, then it becomes very difficult for him to elevate himself spiritually".

"Our thoughts, feelings, beliefs and attitudes can either positively or negatively affect the biological functioning of our body. That means mental health can determine our physical health. Conversely our physical aspects like our eating patterns, exercise, habits, and way of living- all these have a great impact on our mental health or wellbeing. These two in turn influence the spiritual progress that one can achieve in one's life. That means the physical body; mind and spirit are very closely related. The mind- body specialist *Dr. James Gordon* states that our mind and body are inseparable. He says, "The brain and the peripheral nervous system, the endocrine—and immune system and indeed all the organs of our body and all the emotional responses we have, share a common chemical language and are constantly communicating with one another".

"Just as we take nourishing food in appropriate measure and perform exercise and avoid food that are not conducive for good physical health, similarly, we should also take into our mind positive information and practice them and avoid negative and useless information as far as possible so that we can enhance our mental well-being because if one wants to be a good, happy and peaceful human being then it is imperative that he practices positivity, and avoids all negativity in his mind. But usually we do not give as much importance to mind as we give to our body. When the body becomes weak or ill immediately we go to the doctor and get the necessary treatment to get back our physical health. But when the mind becomes weak and negative we do not show the same urgency in giving immediate attention to mind to get rid of its deficiencies and illness that are in the form of negativities. This is where we go wrong. We usually try our level best to make our physical body healthy, attractive and beautiful. We take much effort, spend a lot of time and money and other resources towards this in spite of the fact that some modern beauty treatments may even result in some side effects, or may cause allergy etc. or may harm the body in the long run. But the pity is that we do not take care of our mind as much as we take care of our physical body even though taking proper care of mind and transforming it does not require spending a lot of money and other resources or does not cause adverse results both in the short or in the long run. What is required is only some time for honest self-introspection to know our defects and the determination to weed out the negativities in us and generate positive feelings and thoughts in our mind.

One should understand that our body and mind are closely interrelated as the well-being of one or the lack of it will affect the other also. In fact it is the mental health that to a great extent brings about the physical health of a person. We should know that we the inner self can shine with its original effulgence, with its purity and perfection only when we make our body and particularly and more important, our mind healthy and strong.

If we can get rid of even a single wasteful or negative thought as soon as it gets created in the mind by some method or the other and can fill our mind with positivity then we can say that we have the capacity to win over the evil. No doubt an average worldly man cannot easily prevent negative thoughts entering in to his mind but one should always be in a position to detect such entry and with determination see that a particular negative thought is not allowed to stay there and grow. As soon as a negative tendency enters one's mind he should at once throw it away and fill his mind with some positive thoughts about the same aspect. For example if one sees any negative tendency in another at once he should think about some positive qualities about that person. After all no one is either totally bad or good. Man is a mixture of both. Even the worst man will have some good in him and the goodness in him must be made to occupy our mind whenever we think of any negativity in any other person.

The victory of the good over evil that we come across in all religious stories found in the Hindu *Puranas* make us understand that the good or the positive in us ultimately can win over the devil or the demon or the negativity in us through persistent, continuous, sincere efforts, and with the intervention and help of the divine or God who resides in the beings as the inner self.

In Upanishads in the place of divine or God we find knowledge with the help of which one is able to overpower ignorance or *Maya* that is responsible for all the negativity in man with knowledge or *Gnana* that generates and strengthens positivity in him. When one's mind gets filled with positivity then one becomes that which is divine, pure and perfect inner self that is consciousness, God or Almighty or the Supreme power or the Creator or the Absolute Energy".

"What is the importance of knowledge in attaining peace and happiness in life Swamiji?"

"The scriptures say that we are blind or are unaware of the reality and the reason is our ignorance or lack of pure knowledge or *Gnana*, that makes our mind oscillate between good and bad. Once this ignorance is removed through knowledge then what is real that is imperishable will reveal itself to us- that is, once we remove our ignorance we will come to know that we are neither the body nor the mind, but only the inner spirit, the consciousness, the soul. So according to spirituality once we are able to know the ultimate reality - our original inner self, once we are able to touch our inner core and experience that, that is deep inside us, our inner self that is untainted and without any blemishes and hence pure, then, wisdom or *Vijnana* is bound to result".

"Even in our practical life, with knowledge if we are able to become aware of all that are negative or bad in us and their bad effects and try to remove them with all that are positive, with continuous self-effort, then the goal of peace and happiness can be reached automatically. On the other hand if we continue to be ignorant of our negativity and their bad effects and if we do not make any effort to transform our mind for better then reaching the goal of best possible life will become only a remote possibility and it can never be attained. So it is the light of knowledge that helps us to remove the darkness of our ignorance and make us realize the truth and reach our goal of life".

"Yes it is very true *Swamiji*. It is knowledge that can remove our ignorance. Years before this incident happened. I was put in charge of our college hostel. It was winter time. I was going to the hostel for my usual rounds. It was late in the evening. There were many trees close to each other that looked like a mini forest on either side of the internal road of the spacious campus. The hostel was also a bit farther away from the main gate. One had to go beyond the college building to reach the huge five blocks of the hostel. After entering the campus I was walking towards the hostel. From the spot that I reached, I could only see the sentries at the gate talking to a few workers of the hostel who were going home after their duty. The Sun had almost set. As it was winter season the surrounding had almost become dark. I had covered almost half of the distance to the hostel from the college gate. Except for the chirping of the birds that returned to their nests on the trees there was total silence. Suddenly I felt that somebody was following me. Fear gripped my mind. Even If I had shouted from there it was not possible for anyone to hear me. I did not know what to do. So I began to walk fast. The one behind me also quickened its pace. Then I stood there without moving. Then my follower also stopped at the same time. This I repeated a few times and the result was the same. I began to pray to God intensely for my protection. Then mustering up all my courage and uttering my prayer loudly I suddenly turned back. But to my great relief I did not see anything behind me following me. Then I began to walk turning my face backwards and what did I see there? A dry leaf was sticking to the end portion of my starched sari and when I walked the sari dragged the dry leaf making a strange sound on the cement road and when I stopped walking it also stopped because it was not being dragged by my sari. At once I began to laugh and unable to contain my laughter I sat on a stone bench nearby on my way and laughed and laughed at my ignorance. Anyone who had seen me at that time there sitting and laughing alone would have thought that I had gone mad. If only I had not tried to look back I would have almost fainted on my way. At that moment I realized the truth in the statements of the great spiritual masters that the root of all fear, unhappiness and miseries in the world is due to ignorance and once we are able to remove the darkness of ignorance by bringing the light of knowledge, then wisdom will dawn on us".

"Yes; exactly. That means one should always try to obtain the necessary knowledge to remove all his ignorance. Without removing ignorance nothing can be achieved in this world. The necessary knowledge one can get only by self-analysis. Even the one who is full of negativity can transform his mind and acquire positivity by proper awareness and self-enquiry provided he has the desire and will to transform himself for reaping the benefits of positivity. What is required is the removal of ignorance by obtaining the needed knowledge and become positive by imbibing as many virtues as possible. This alone will make man lead a life of happiness and peace in this world and also make his life worthy and purposeful which is the very goal of human life".

" If one analyses one's nature he will come to know where he stands and what his negativities are, why they are cropping up, what are its harmful consequences, what is to be done for reaping good beneficial results, how to change his nature and so on. Then he is bound to create in himself as many virtues as possible. After all nothing is impossible for a willing heart. Where there is a will there is a way. With determination one can bring about changes in his past accumulated tendencies also. Humans have such capacity to adopt and adapt themselves. There is immense potential in man and with determination and effort if he taps his potential then he can transform and elevate his mind to reap good for himself as well as for the others. He should not allow negativity to enter into his mind and if it creeps in he should try to eliminate them immediately with positivity. He should also not allow the negativity of the others or of the situations affect him at all. Both these are possible only when he cultivates positivity in himself with the necessary knowledge."

"One should understand his thoughts, emotions and feelings, become aware of his negativity, its source and its solution; remove the negative feelings with positive ones; know, remember and practice all positive values of life; follow any path towards holistic health and listen to his own inner voice but not the mind that is very tricky, and choose the right path by taking the correct decision with the help of the discriminating ability of the brain. It is also a maxim that nothing worthwhile can be accomplished easily and without effort. So why not make an attempt and get the best out of life and make life a real celebration? We know only about our present life. Even for the one who believes in rebirth the past is gone forever and the future is yet to come as we cannot know about either of our past or our future births experientially. Only our present life is a reality as far as we are concerned. So why can't we take care of our present life and make it the best possible so that the future will take care of itself? So instead of wasting time in thinking about our past or about the future we should concentrate on our present and make our life the most, happy and peaceful by making our lives worthy and purposeful. We have to help ourselves in creating the best possible life for us because others cannot give us that".

"A well-known fact that is revealed by religion, spirituality as well as science is that no energy can be lost but can only change its form. Negative energy can be converted in to positive energy with positive thoughts and also by lessening negativity and strengthening positivity in us. The same is the case with negative thoughts that create negative energy that weaken our body, mind and spirit. It is also an accepted fact that everything that we radiate or send out will come back to us sooner or later with more force and intensity- whether it is positive or negative. So, positive thoughts will return to us with even more power; so also negative thoughts. It is because similar thoughts attract similar feelings and emotions. That means every thought is like a seed that already has in it in potential form the corresponding tree in itself.

The negativity or the positivity in us is also the result of our past negativity or positivity that go back to several births of ours. What we sow we have to reap over a period of time. Some may yield the result quickly while other thoughts may take a longer duration of time to reveal their result since there cannot be any effect without a cause. However man who is endowed with intelligence and knowledge is also endowed with the power and freedom to choose either the good or bad. Because of this capacity man is in a position to create all that are good or positive for himself and for the others and with that eliminate all the bad or negative that is in him to a great extent. That is why it is said that it is we who can make our future-our destiny".

"Thank you very much Swamiji. If I am not wasting your time and if I am not causing inconvenience to you, can I ask you some more questions? Will you please answer them?"

Why not? We are here only to help people like you who come and seek answers for questions and ask for clarifications. It is our duty. Go ahead with all your questions without any hesitation" said the *Swamiji.*

3

Negativity

"Swamiji , "You said one should remove as many negatives in him as possible. Before you start telling me about how we can remove our negativity I would like to know something more about its nature".

The *Swamiji* began, "Negative qualities are like weeds. They need neither fertile soil nor manure to grow. They also grow in plenty and it is very difficult to weed them out totally. Even when they are removed they will continue to grow until their very roots are plucked. No one will ever want to cultivate weeds just because they grow without any effort and will grow in plenty. All will only desire to put in maximum effort to cultivate good plants that would yield flowers and fruits that are useful to man. The negativity in man also is like this. They are highly destructive and ruinous. They do not require any attention or effort on the part of any one to grow as they are such that they will grow even without our notice, attention or effort. In fact, like the weeds they will grow more if one does not pay any attention to it- even if one does not desire to nurture it. Similarly, if one does not pay attention to negativity, and is not careful enough then they will grow in plenty and will spoil the very life of the person. If the weeds are not removed constantly then it will affect the very growth of the plants that one wishes to grow. Similarly constant alertness on the part of one in detecting the very appearance of the weeds of negativity in his mind and quick removal of such weeds namely the negative thoughts, emotions or feelings as soon as they appear in one's mind and filling the place by planting good plants of positive feelings, thoughts or emotions is what is required for one to make his life happy, peaceful, purposeful and worthy. On the other hand if one does not care to pluck the weeds of negative thoughts that are arising in his mind and instead if he nourishes and encourages such thoughts then he is sure to make his life miserable and unworthy and very soon he will become a personification of all that are negative and will get addicted to such tendencies that will ruin not only his present life but also his subsequent births as his mind will carry the negative tendencies as long as they exist in his mind, that is as long as he experiences repeated births and deaths unless he removes them with his own self effort."

"Swamiji, kindly tell me about the qualities that can be categorized as negative. Although I have some idea I would like to hear that from your mouth. It will be enough if you can list out a few negative qualities in man".

"Expectations, ill will, hurt, clinging and brooding over the past and anxiety about the future, self-pity, thoughts of destruction, anxiety, false sympathy, jealousy, thoughts of exploiting others, aggressiveness, fury, torment, frustration, suicidal tendencies, possessiveness, greed, selfish thoughts, depression, enmity, vengeance, pessimism, hostility, fear, worry, restlessness, sadness, loneliness, anger, rudeness, delusion, nervousness, dullness, stress, boredom, resentment, hatred, bitterness, envy, selfish and self-centered thoughts, pessimism, hostility, irritation, anxiety, loneliness, irritability, apathy, discontentment, violence, anti-social tendencies, self-destructive behavior, cheating, dejection, disillusionment etc. are some of the examples of negative thoughts and emotions and feelings.

Sri Krishna in His *Bhagavad Gita* calls people with negative tendencies devilish. He says that these are people who exhibit hypocrisy, arrogance, self- conceit, pride, harshness, anger and ignorance etc. In fact all those emotions and thoughts that do not contribute to the mental as well as physical well-being of any one and that of the others can be categorized as negative. All such emotions, thoughts, words and actions contribute for the negativity of a person and these generate an unhappy, restless feeling in one because of the negative energy in oneself. This negative energy he passes on to others through the negative vibrations that are radiated from him who is filled with such energy. The ancient Indian scriptures mention six broad categories of negative qualities that they termed as internal enemies of man. These are, *Kama* or lust, *Krodha* or anger, *Lobha* or greed, *Moha* or illusion and emotional attachment, *Mada* or *Ahamkar* that is pride and *Matsarya* that is envy or jealousy. Since most of us experience all these or some of these negative feelings and also because these are to be wiped out from our minds these negativities or vices need not be elaborated upon as we should concentrate our attention in eliminating these thoughts as soon as they crop up in our mind".

"What is the source of negativity Swamiji"?

"There are innumerable negative thoughts and emotions that lead to negative expressions and also actions. However to tackle all these individually is a great task and it may also be impossible. So the best way to tackle all problems of negativity whether it is found in oneself, or in others or in situations is to know their root cause.

Actually the problem does not lie with any outside factors-individuals or situations and so on. The problem lies in our own perception and attitudes. Most of the negative feelings and thoughts that lead to negativity can be prevented and avoided if only we are in a position to bring about the necessary required changes in our perception as well as attitudes towards others and towards situations in life. When we view something or some situation as bad or not happy for us then we generate negative emotions like anger, frustration, self- pity, pain, worry, tension, stress etc. in ourselves".

"Negativity is seen in one because one perceives negativity mainly in others or in situations. The root cause for such a perception is one's sense of ego that leads to attachment and expectations on the one hand and his desire or craving on the other. These two arise in the mind of man due to ignorance that is lack of proper knowledge. The ancient sages of India denoted this ignorance as Maya. If any one's words or actions or if any situation boosts one's ego then he becomes happy and he gets all positive feelings towards that person or situations. On the other hand if one is being criticized or if any other person does not accept or agree his viewpoints then one's ego gets hurt and that generates negativity in him. But we should know that the nature of each person is different. Even twins differ in their qualities. If that is so then how can we expect others to behave as we want them to behave? And it is also not possible for us to behave as per the wishes and expectations of the others. We cannot expect others to follow us, be like us. It will only create disappointments and negative feelings in us. Suppose you appreciate somebody for speaking, or doing in a certain manner. Then you expect the other person also to appreciate you in the same manner and when it does not happen you get upset, irritated and you are angry and you start hating the other person because your ego does not get boosted. Suppose you have no expectation from the other then the negative qualities also will not find a place in you. Intense desire is another root cause of several other types of negativity. If one sees that some other person is better off than him, in looks, personality, in position, riches etc. or when some other who competes with him gets something that he himself failed to achieve then also the desire for that makes him send out negative energy to the other person. Numerous such examples can be given from our day to day experience. So if one is able to tackle the problem that lies within himself then he can go a long way in reducing negativity to a remarkable extent.

Desire is a natural trait in beings and is good because it is the motivating factor for all success, development, improvement, innovations or discovery and so on and so forth in one's life. But if desire for material things becomes craving that is uncontrollable then one goes to any extent to get or to achieve what he craves for and this leads to undesirable and unhealthy competition, hatred, jealousy, greed and so on. Similarly, egoism, that is, the feeling of 'I' we find in any worldly person. But too much of egoism will result in over confidence, pride etc. that will destroy the very life of a person. It will also lead to expectations. These are certainly negative tendencies that do no good. So one should be cautious enough and keep his sense of ego and his desires within limits so that negative thoughts do not crop up in his mind first of all."

"Swamiji, will you kindly tell me how negativity affects the physical and mental health of a person?"

"Negative thoughts are highly depressive, destructive and harmful both to the sender and also the receiver of such thoughts as they create negative energy in both that destroy happiness and peace for both. Physical diseases are to a great extent connected to our attitudes, emotions and our mental makeup. So to enjoy a good physical health, it is imperative that one is also mentally healthy. For a strong mental health one should have as much positivity and as little negativity as possible.

Negative emotions cause disease, illness and premature aging because emotions are a form of energy that runs through our body and mind. Each emotion has its own vibration. Our bodies respond to different thoughts and feelings. Negative feelings create stress in our body and through certain kind of chemical reactions in the body they lead to physical illness. Negative thoughts, emotions and feelings are found to be very harmful to the body as it arrests the harmonious flow of energy. These create blocks of resistance in our body. To be more specific, such thoughts and emotions lead to cardio vascular diseases, ulcers, blood pressure, headaches, and respiratory problems and so on. On the other hand positive qualities result in the relaxation of the body contributing to both physical and mental well- being. It is found that the central nervous system executes orders both automatically and also at the level of mind, that is the thought process. For example the functioning of heart, liver, stomach, lungs etc. are no doubt automatic but their functions can be lowered or accelerated through mind. When a person is in fear or in an angry mood then his heart beat rises up where as when he is relaxed and calm his heart beat slows down. Anger is also a sign of heart disease and it may also result in heart problems. Also it has been proved that negative attitudes contain toxins that damage the vital organs of the body like liver. Negativity also creates stress in the body and increases the blood pressure and heart beat. Our breath becomes short, shallow, quick. The acidity in the stomach increases causing ulcer in the stomach. All these lead to weak immune system resulting in all physical diseases. It is said that negativity even changes the color and texture of our skin. It has been proved that the negative feelings induce diseases of heart, liver, kidney, spleen and stomach. It is found to damage the brain cells, throw poisonous chemical products into the blood, suppresses the secretion of gastric juice, bile and other digestive juices in the alimentary canal. It is also found that negativity drains and depletes our energy and vitality and induces premature old age in one."

"When both mind and body are agitated due to negative feelings, emotions and thoughts then the *Prana* or the inner energy will flow in an unequal manner instead of flowing equally all over the body. This will result in unrythmic vibration of energy in the whole body causing diseases both physical as well as psychological. Calmness of mind is therefore very important both for the physical and mental wellbeing that automatically bring the spiritual wellbeing in man".

"It is also found that as the current of an emotion travels in our body it triggers the release of chemical proteins called Neuro-Peptides. Each emotion is supposed to have a different frequency. These tiny chemical proteins create physiological response. The body produces many different neuro-Peptide and each controls different physiological functions and each neuro-Peptide create certain physiological response. Adrenalin releases when we experience fear, anxiety, or stress. It also results in the dilatation of blood vessels and makes the skin flush and there is rapid, shallow breathing. Especially around the stomach and shoulder area the muscles tighten up and we experience slight to moderate or even heavy sweating at such times. Adrenalin makes the body to be in a highly alert state. No doubt it is helpful in emergencies but over a long period of time Adrenalin can become very damaging to the physical health. It is found that it damages the immune system, slows down digestion, uses up vital vitamins and minerals, causes pain and stiffness, makes our body acidic and results in inflammation and drains the vitality of the body. Adrenalin is also highly addictive as the body gets accustomed to over stimulation in course of time and the body needs it more and more of it to maintain higher energy levels.

Studies have also proved that negative emotions damage and weaken our physical body and its strength. The negative emotions also leave a permanent scar on our body by disrupting the natural flow of energy causing depletion of our energy. Recent studies have shown that loneliness spurs production of Proteins that signals the presence of inflammation linked to coronary heart diseases, type-2 Diabetes, Arthritis and Alzheimer's disease and frailty and functional decline in old people. Negative energy also induces more and more negativity in one. It also makes the mind restless without any peace and one is unable to take correct decisions at such times and what all he thinks, speaks or does go wrong"

"People with significant negativity encounter only problems but not solutions for the problems. Any negative emotion reflects on our face and the expressions on our face. It also makes our mind to focus on outcomes that are adverse and which we do not desire to happen in our life. It makes our life heavy, miserable and unhappy with no peace of mind. We become desperate and helpless because at such moments we see only problems, failures and dangers everywhere."

"Buddha said that holding on to anger is like grasping a hot coal with the intention of throwing it at someone else- but you are the one getting burns. It is like taking poison and wishing that the other person would die on account of that. It is also said that "Neither a sharp sword nor an infuriated serpent is so much killing as anger that resides in our own minds". If you are patient in one moment of anger, you will avoid one hundred days of sorrow says a Chinese proverb. It is found that resentment and bitterness are supposed to be like acid and cause inflammation and pain. Any bottled up hurt results in Arthritis. Back pain is found to be the result of a feeling of lack of support. Medulla back pain is caused by carrying the weight of the past; Thoracic back pain is because of the feeling of lack of love or emotional support , an imbalance between the rational mind and emotions causes digestive upsets, constipation, diarrhea and similar digestive disorders and so on. Any negative attitude brings about physical and mental problems there by makes one physically and mentally ill. We also know that negative thoughts arrest the self-healing efforts when we are ill. But all of us want only a good physical and mental well-being and the secret of mental and physical health requires least negativity and maximum positivity in us".

"Walking barefoot on grass, more physical activities that takes extra oxygen for deep breath that is required after exercise, meditation, that brings about calmness and balance between the right and left hemispheres of the brain, prayer, selfless work or service, and awareness of the negativity in us and practicing virtues are some of the ways to minimize them and come out of any negativity in us.

Just as even a single disease that affects our body if is not treated properly may lead to a lot of problems for maintaining a good physical health similarly if we ignore any single negative emotion or feeling in us then it will cause immense damage to our mental and physical health. So as soon as we detect any negativity in us we should analyze the cause of it and find out proper remedy or solution to wipe away such thought completely from our mind. The study of impact of emotions on our physical and mental health has given rise to the emergence of a new field of medicine, the 'energy psychology' in modern times."

"Now I understand that negative emotions damage our mental and physical wellbeing. Tell me how we can tackle the problem of negativity?"

"With proper and clear understanding it is possible to reduce negativity to a great extent. First of all we should not get identified ourselves with negativity. We must know that they are different from us and that they relate to our perception and attitude. One must also accept the fact that it is not possible for any being to have everything according to the way he wants, according to our liking or everyone to behave in the way we want them to behave. So before we think or say or do anything we must take time to observe our thoughts, emotions, attitude and feelings and identify that particular emotion in us that tries to take an upper hand. We must take time to analyze that particular emotion. Sometimes when positive emotions dominate we sour to greater heights or levels of all that are positive. So also, in the case of negative emotions we sometimes go down to the bottommost level and inflict pain to ourselves and also for the others. At such times our emotional mind by passes the intelligence that has the power of discretion and without analyzing the consequences properly we say something or do something revealing the negativity in us. So, one should not act spontaneously especially when negative tendencies come up in our mind. We must try to understand that any emotion is not lasting but only temporary and then try to get over it. That is why it is said that when you want to do good and positive things then you should do it immediately then and there without any postponement because after some time you may not want to do it especially because there is possibility that you become selfish when the heat of the emotion die away. But when any negative feelings come to us it is better that we do not react or even respond to it immediately in an impulsive manner, instead we should try to calm down ourselves and should refrain from uttering or doing anything at that moment. After sometime the emotion will disappear and we will only brush it aside as the intensity of our negative emotions gradually come down and we longer will care to react. For example when any one harms us we should not react and try to pay him in the same coin. We have to brush it aside with the knowledge that one's actions only reveal his *Samskaras* or his inherent tendencies. Mahatma Gandhi stated, "Be the change you seek". One should refrain from blaming others or situations for one's negativity. It is only escapism. We should also never allow negativity in ourselves or in others or in situations to overpower and weaken us. Instead, along with safeguarding ourselves from negativity from the outside we should also prevent negativity getting generated in our own mind. As far as possible, one should also try to give support and love to those who are faced with negative emotions by helping them in a friendly way to get out of their negativity. We should also empower ourselves in such a way that we do not create any type of negativity even if the situations are adverse to us. Further, we should also acknowledge the fact that life is a mixture of both good and bad and empower ourselves with positivity so that we can drive away any type of negative feeling that tries to enter into our mind. All the negatives in the world will fail to affect that person whose mind is under his own control so that even if any negative thoughts comes up in his mind he will find ways and means to remove them by his own efforts so that he can make himself and the others enjoy happiness and peace".

"There should be vigilant self-analysis and self-monitoring and also awareness so that one can check and safeguard himself from the generation of any negative thoughts in his mind. For this one should always be conscious of all his negative thoughts words and actions. Whenever any negative thought comes to our mind we should immediately cut it off or curb them because dwelling on negativity will only empower itself helping none in the process. If we can practice this constantly then we will be able to minimize our negative feelings and emotions to a great extent so that we can make our life happy, peaceful, worthy and purposeful".

"However one should not think badly about oneself because he has negativity. This will create only a low self-esteem in him that again will encourage negativity in him. Negativity in return for negativity also should never be our motto as this will only add to the already existing negative energy in one. We should never try to suppress our negative feelings because such efforts will only strengthen the negativity in us. So with conscious effort one should become aware of one's negativity and their harmful effects on himself and others, determine not to repeat them and practice what he has determined and also fill his mind with as much positivity as possible so that the negativity in him will go away on its own".

"Just as we wash our body regularly with soap and water for cleaning and removing the dirt on the body we have to cleanse our mind regularly, every moment, again and again with positivity whenever the dirt of negativity makes its appearance in our mind. This only can make our mind devoid of negativity at any point of time. For this one should always be vigilant and catch hold of the dirt of negativity as soon as it enters into our mind. No doubt even immediately after a process of cleaning the mind, negativity may come up in our mind again. Then it is our duty to detect such negativities every time they crop up and wash off the negativity from our mind with positivity. Such a process of cleaning must go on and on and then gradually the number of negative thoughts and emotions of our mind will get reduced automatically in course of time. The ordinary worldly beings can tackle the problem of negativity in this manner".

"The spiritual aspirants go still further and they tackle the problem of negativity by keeping their senses under their control so that the senses do not indulge in objects and people outside themselves unnecessarily. Instead they turn their attention inward through meditation, prayer, or selfless work that will result in lofty sacred positive thoughts and feelings. All desires of the mind crop up once the sense organs, the *jnanendriyas* come into contact with the outside world and this result in good or bad perception and the bad ones become the negative emotions. Still at a higher level the spiritually elevated souls discard all the desires of their body and mind automatically without any effort as they have realized that the fundamental cause that is the main root of all problems of negativity lies in desires of man. These great ones know fully well that it is desire that makes man turn his mind and body towards the world through their senses that causes all hardship for man. Once the desires are fulfilled man becomes restless and in tension as he has to safeguard all that he had amassed or achieved in worldly life. This creates tension and anxiety, etc. in him. On the other hand if he is unable to achieve his heart's desires then he becomes sad or angry for not getting what he wanted and it also creates jealousy in him for those who could obtain or achieve what he could not. They therefore do not allow the desires for worldly things and people to subjugate them. But this may not be possible for all ordinary humans. What best they can do is to know these facts and be guarded against desires that try to overpower them, keep their senses under their control and view things in a positive manner as far as possible".

"Swamiji, There are times we get affected when we perceive negativity in the others. How are we to safeguard ourselves from the effects of such negativity?"

"As I told you already, all negative thoughts are harmful both to the person who releases them and to those who receive them. It will deplete the energy of both the sender as well as the recipient. Negative thoughts send out negative energy. It affects the sender more than the recipient because it affects and generates negative energy in the other only when he is mentally affected by such negative feelings of the sender of such thoughts".

"When the person on whom it is targeted is not aware of the negative emotions of the sender or when he is indifferent to any such emotions on the part of the sender of the negative energy or when the stored up positive energy due to positivity of the recipient of the negative thought is at a higher level then, no negativity targeted at one can affect that person and therefore no negative energy will get generated in him and there is no depletion of energy in him. On the other hand if one becomes aware of the negative emotions sent to him by another, and when one is very sensitive and takes it to his heart the negative attitude of the other person or when the stored up positive energy in one is less than the intensity of the negative energy sent by the other person then automatically the recipient gets affected by that and consequently he will experience a lot of depletion of energy in him and he becomes unhappy and restless even without his own knowing, the negative energy will get piled up in him even though he on his own is not responsible for such generation of negativity in him. So one should have enough and more positive attitudes that generate positive energy in him, so that, he will be able to face and also overpower the negativity of the other person. This is the best defense that one can have to safeguard oneself from any attack of negative emotions of the other. This is possible only when we make our mind as positive as possible for us so that we do not get subjugated by the negativity that we perceive as being targeted at us by some other person."

"When someone projects negativity at another, for example when somebody insults the other one need not take it personally. Either they may not be aware of the negativity in them and how it affects the others or they may be people who have negative attitudes to everything and everyone they come across. They are born critics. Such people are like those affected by jaundice. To a person who is affected by jaundice everything looks yellow. Similarly one who has more negativity than positivity in him will find only negativity everywhere and in every person and in every situation so he automatically projects negative tendencies. There are also a few who cherish and enjoy negativity without knowing its consequences either immediately or in the long run. Such people have a closed mind. They think that their own perception is right or good and proper. It is very difficult for such people to improve themselves. So, the one who becomes the target of such a person's negativity should ignore the negative emotions, words and actions of the sender of negative energy. One should not pay any attention to such negativity as there is no need to give any value or importance to such behavior. Such a response without any reaction will also gradually make the sender of negative emotions analyze his own nature at some time or the other in his life time because none will like and love such a person and all will only try to avoid the very presence and nearness of such a one. This will make him realize his negative behavior one day or the other and he himself will try to transform himself at least to make him lovable to the others".

"There are also cases when we misunderstand people and get negative feelings about them. This happens when one jumps into conclusions before understanding the other person properly. Such types of negativities can be prevented by not trying to judge others at all. It is wrong to judge any one, including ourselves".

"It is also beneficial if one can spend more time with optimistic, positive people who radiate positivity. Spending more time with cynical people with negative emotions will radiate negative energy all around them and it will also make the others more and more negative. So it is better to be far away from such people physically and mentally as far as possible".

"One can also cultivate the let go attitude towards the negativity of the others. As far as possible we should forget, forgive and ignore any negative attitude of the others in a broadminded manner and just move on without giving any importance to them. This attitude on one's part will help one in protecting himself from the negativity of the others. It will help us in not having any negative feelings towards the one who happens to target negativity at us. As *Gandhiji* said, an eye for an eye only ends up making the whole world blind. For example, when you know that somebody is exploiting you, because you are kind or broadminded etc. then give some margin to their actions. We should understand that their negativity is because they are weak due to their negative energy. This will make us pity them and help them if possible with positivity, humility and sympathy. Allow them to exploit you although you are quite aware of it and show that you do not mind it. When we play with children don't we let ourselves get defeated deliberately to make the children happy? But when your goodness is taken as weakness by them continuously then it is better to withdraw from such people totally. However we should not return negativity for negativity. If we do so we are only degrading ourselves to their level. At the same time we also should not exploit others by taking advantage of their, age, sex, position or goodness, circumstances and so on. Imagine yourself in their position. Then you will never want to exploit anybody in this world".

"One should analyze as to why any outside negativity should affect him at all in the first place. It is up to one to choose the way one wants to be and whether to react, respond, get affected or ignore the negativity of another. If one gets angry at another person the other person also need not in turn get angry at all. Only weak minded people with an unstable mind with a dependent nature give importance and get affected due to other's negativity at them. Such a person's happiness or sorrow depends too much upon the other person's attitude and behavior. It only reveals one's weakness and dependent nature. Such a state of mind will be burdensome both for oneself as well as for the others, especially in the case of intimate relationships. Just as a person who is endowed with a strong body is very independent and he does not depend upon the others much because he is self- sufficient and is able to do most of the things by himself without any dependence on any other person, similarly one who is endowed with a strong and healthy mind does not get affected by the negativity of the others because he is mentally quite independent. Mahatma Gandhi said that nobody can hurt him without his permission. Such was his mental, moral strength".

"There are times when we cannot avoid our physical presence during any negative acts or expression of negative feelings of another, then under such circumstances we can at least switch off our mind by turning our mind to some other thoughts that give us some positive feeling. If one has a strong mind then he will maintain his cool and will never get perturbed or affected whatever may be the intensity of the negative emotions of the other. He will just be indifferent to the other person's negativity by switching off his mind at that moment, or by not giving any importance to the other person who projects his negativity through his words and actions. When the only alternative to protect yourself from the negativity of others is to distance yourself from them, then it must be done not by hating the other person but only to protect yourself from the negative vibrations of the other. Such a response from you may also make the other person cool down and repent for his negativity".

"One may also try to understand the other person in an objective manner. It is possible that the other person is mentally or physically upset or irritated over some issue and his negativity in all probability might be the result of that. This knowledge will create sympathy towards the other person who initially sent the negative vibrations and at the same time will safeguard one from other's negativity".

"One can also tolerate any negativity in the other person, especially in the case of intimate relationships, with the belief that perhaps he had done something similar to that in the past in any of his intimate relationships either in that birth or in some other earlier births and it is only inevitable that he becomes the target of the negativity in his present birth. But such thoughts should come to him without any self-pity or any feeling of hurt for himself. This will not only enable him to protect himself from the negativity of the other but will also pave the way for his self-improvement and he will determine to become more and more positive and less and less negative. But if one does not have such a mindset then it is better to be aloof from such people who project negativity. If your role as a partner or as a parent does not allow you to distance yourself physically then you may distance yourself mentally from such onslaughts of negativity".

"Sometimes the negative behavior of the other towards us may also be the consequence of our negative behavior towards them. So if one wants to prevent negativity from the other then he should refrain from his own negative emotions or feelings and behavior. This requires a continuous self-introspection of one's thoughts, words that he had uttered and his actions and understanding of one's own drawbacks. Without stopping there one should also rectify his mistakes by not allowing negative thoughts in his mind, not uttering negative words that hurt others and not acting in such a manner that may cause hardship to others. Such a change in him will not only make him lovable to all the others but will also make him enjoy happiness and peace within himself".

It is also possible that one may counteract the attacks of negativity from the other with positivity, whatever may be the magnitude and intensity of such negativity. Just as light removes darkness automatically, positive emotions are bound to remove the negative tendencies in any man. If one makes a sarcastic remark about one's features or height or colour then the other by taking it in a light jovial manner can safeguard himself from the negative feelings against the other who has passed such comments. Similarly if one tries to push or pull another deliberately then one can merely smile at the other or may pat the shoulder of the other in a very friendly manner. This will make the other person to feel ashamed of himself. This is the best method for the one who is physically weak than the other who attacked him. But if one causes any considerable physical harm to another to show off his superiority or arrogance then it is necessary to teach him a lesson though not in the same measure just to make him realize that that it is not your weakness but your broadmindedness and goodness that made you pocket his negative words and actions. This holds good only in the case of one who possesses superior physical strength when compared to the attacker. But this should be the last option and even if such a measure is adopted it should be done without any ill will or hatred for the other person".

"Is it humanly possible to project positivity in return for the attack of negativity of the others towards us, Swamiji? And even if one returns negativity of the other with positivity will he not be considered as weak minded and will he not be exploited in the world?"

"No doubt such a response is not easy and it is possible only for the enlightened souls. In our worldly life the one who returns smile for a frown, softness for rudeness, love for hatred, kindness for unkindness, and broadmindedness for narrow-mindedness and humility for arrogance etc. are very rare and it is also a fact that such people in all likelihood will be considered by the others, especially in the modern world as weak who can merely pocket everything and anything because that one is not strong enough mentally or physically and is intelligent enough to understand the negativity in the other person and protect himself by reacting to the negativity through words or actions. But the reality is that only weak minded unintelligent people react quickly and in a hasty manner and they get upset and perturbed over any type of negative attacks on them because they have a feeling that if they do not return negativity for negativity in the same measure then they will be laughed at by others. But then why should anybody bother about other's impressions about us. The one who has control over his mind will only ignore any type of negativity aimed at him. He will also never bother about others' impressions about him under such circumstances. He, in a broadminded manner will respond negativity with a greater measure of positivity and this is the most magnanimous way to protect oneself from the onslaughts of negativity. By such acts one becomes the lord of any situation and nobler and far greater than the other person who sent the negative energy and in all probability, that person who projected negativity is bound to feel ashamed for his negative behavior and he will also get the necessary inspiration for his self-improvement because such acts will touch the very core of his heart that is the seat of all emotions".

"Sometimes when we respond negativity with positivity it triggers more negativity in the other person. What is the solution then?"

"Yes. Sometimes in the case of some people, when you utter positive words for any negative ones the other may become more stubborn or he may continue to be more and more negative especially if he is proud and egoistic person. This is especially so in moods like anger. This will only worsen the situation. But continuous positive acts may cool down the other person at least gradually. At such times one should act silently in a positive manner. Although in the beginning stages there may not be any response, continuous persistent positive actions of the affected one will cool down the other person gradually. Sooner or later he will understand his negativity and will try to follow the other."

"Some people resort to temporary measures like drinking alcohol etc. to forget their feelings of hurt, suffering, pain, unhappiness and so on in spite of the fact that these measures surely, harm their body and mind in the long run. What about such a response Swamiji"?

"Even when one becomes very unhappy or miserable or depressed on account of some other's negativity or due to highly unfavorable or even sad situations and so on one should not divert his attention from the resultant negativity by some alternative measures like smoking, drinking etc. These are only temporary measures that make him forget what he does not want to remember and it will also spoil his physical and mental health. After the effect of that particular diversion is over the feeling of hurt or anger or agony etc. will come up on the surface of his mind as such methods cannot wipe out or eliminate negativity. So the best way to eliminate negativity of this type is to generate positive feelings in our mind continuously so that positivity will get deep rooted in our mind."

"One should also train himself to recognize the positivity in another whenever the other person projects negativity. It is a great art. When someone criticizes us then we must take it as an opportunity to examine and know our weaknesses. For example, when someone who is in an angry mood says that you are the worst possible human being on earth, then take this remark as an opportunity to detect your own weaknesses or negativity. When you are in the midst of people who always praise you, appreciate and admire you then you get no opportunity to know about your own negativity and make an effort to reduce or eliminate it. Only criticism will make you think more about yourself and your own mistakes or defects in you. No one likes criticisms. They are bitter for everyone. But many a time one is able to improve himself because he is being criticized."

"One may also try to find out the areas where one is in agreement with the other who projects some negativity at him by trying to understand the other person's view points and highlight the positivity in the other. Such a step will make the other person to deal with you with an open heart. This will make that person find in you a friend who can share his views".

"Thus it is clear that the best way to protect ourselves from the negativity of others is to bring about the desired changes in ourselves because we have no control on the emotions of others however close they may be. No one wants to be dictated by the other. Changing others is also not possible. Even children follow the advice of the parents only when they are convinced. Mere preaching on the part of parents can never bring about the desired changes in their children. They can make their children listen to their advices only if they practice what they preach. When that is the case how can we ever imagine changing others"?

"Certain situations in our life also create negativity in us. How are we to protect ourselves from such negativity Swamiji?"

"Sometimes negative energy builds up in one because of situations that he considers as negative, undesirable and unhappy and not conducive for him and so on. At such times we do not even spare God from blaming. We feel that we are being punished for no fault of ours or we wonder why God has targeted and chosen us only of all the people for such a situation. Many people even lose all their faith in God when they are faced with extremely negative and adverse situations that is a fatal blow to them financially or emotionally or health wise. Many a time even the objects or for that matter even the time factor also are the targets of our negativity. For example if a machine does not work properly, if there is a traffic block while we are travelling to reach a particular place at the earliest, or if we are unable to finish a work by ourselves or by the others on time then in all these circumstances also we get unnecessarily irritated, upset and we get angry in an irrational manner. These are the times when we have to take things for granted, accept the situations as they are and move on without any negativity in us as building of negativity can never change the situation. On the other hand it will result in lots of depletion of positive energy in us. We must understand that just as we have no control on others we have no control over many of the situations of life. The negativity or the feeling of anger, depression, disappointments and the like that one feels when he comes across any adverse situation that gives rise to negative feeling can be tackled by finding out the positive side of such situations. One should consider any situation that brings about negative feeling in one like sorrow, misery, disappointment, depression etc. by taking such situations as a test of his courage and mental strength and instead of brooding over that he must find ways to overcome such situations so that he does not get trapped in negativity. We must also know that we cannot control what goes on outside ourselves and what is beyond our control. So the best way is to control that that is inside us.

It is also a fact that everything in this world is relative. Whenever anyone has to face any negative situations in his life he can overcome the feeling of negativity in him by imagining a worse situation than that one that he faces at any point of time. That will give him some peace. Because man always prefers a bad situation to a worse or even worst situation. Such a thought process will make him thank God or his stars or the situation because he knows that situation could have become even worse or the worst possible.

When any situation brings him a fatal blow one should try to eliminate the negativity that is arising in his mind. It is natural for humans to feel extremely sad, dejected, depressed and so on whenever he has to face a situation that gives him a fatal blow. But with awareness one should patiently bear everything calmly and accept such a situation as he cannot bring any change in that situation. Allowing and entertaining negativity even at such times will only bring more and more unhappiness to him and to those who are near and dear to him. It will also create more and more negative energy in him and others resulting in physical and mental ill health to one and all without serving any purpose".

"There are also situations when one is dragged in to a certain situation that one does not like at all. Under such circumstances one has to remain calm and cool and non- committal without getting involved or even associated with such situations. If it is possible then he can protect himself from any consequent negativity by distancing himself from such situations both physically and mentally as well.

Some situations we may not be able to avoid from happening. So the best way is to accept the situations as they are, and if possible try to understand the positive side of it in the short run or in the long run or to find ways and means to overcome such unpleasant and unwanted situations through one's own efforts, or accept such situations calmly with the understanding that what cannot be cured must be endured patiently, without any complaint or self-pity because whatever has to happen will happen and even if we try our level best we may not be able to avoid them. At best we can only try to forget and try to erase from our memory such situations that have resulted in great hardship or misery to us."

"So what you say is, negativity arises in us because we perceive bad in others and situations and so it must be we who can find the necessary solution. Is it not Swamiji?"

"Exactly. Actually it is not the people or situations that create positive or negative thoughts in us giving rise to positive or negative feelings, emotions, words or acts. Problems arise in our mind and also settle in our mind. So it is the patient who suffers the disease as well as cures the disease. The problem therefore is not with the outside world. Because we do not get what we expected from others or situations of life we get negativities in our mind that result in our unhappiness and misery. On the other hand if we see the same thing with the opposite view then everything will seem pleasant and positive to us. So it is ignorance that makes us think that our happiness lies with things, people and situations outside ourselves. Actually these give neither happiness nor misery for man because it is our way of thinking and understanding that either creates positive or negative feelings in us. So we are actually responsible for our negativity and we only can change our perception from being negative to positive. So we are our own problems and our own solutions. If that is so why should we allow ourselves to entertain bad or negative thoughts? And even if we get such thoughts why can't we get over them and fill ourselves with positive thoughts through self-awareness? This is the question that we have to ask ourselves and find out the answer also by ourselves because one can uplift one's mind only by sincere, persistent effort with awareness of the root of the problem and its solution. But then why should we perceive anything or any person or events or situations as negative at all? It is because of one's own ignorance of the ultimate reality that actually there is neither good nor bad in this world. Good and bad, positive and negative arise only because of the difference in our perception. That is why what is positive to one becomes negative for the other and even for the same person that which was negative before becomes positive later. But this awareness comes only for great men of wisdom. For those who are worldly and with varied responsibilities to fulfill there is bound to be the distinction of good and bad.

People do get negative feelings and emotions due to others and also due some adverse situations of life and also because of their own negativity. But one must try to eliminate the negativities arising in his mind at such times through the knowledge that it is we who create the negative feelings because of our own perceptions and if we are able to change our perception and see only positivity everywhere then our life will be beautiful.

However there are certain situations in one's life when negative feelings like pain, misery, disappointments, and dejection and so on may arise. For example in the case of a serious injury, in the case of death of near and dear ones, in the case of major failures and setbacks in one's life one is bound to get negative feelings. But then one must ask oneself, what he can do to change the situation or outcome. If it is in his hands to change the situation then he must try his best to change the situation or happening so that he will not generate any negative tendencies in him. But if any situation like death of a close relative or any natural calamity like floods or earthquakes when one loses everything that belongs to him or when one faces great set back in one's life, -all these have to be borne patiently without complaint or self-pity or despair and this is the only solution. But then people attain this stage only after undergoing a lot of negative tendencies like self-pity and misery and so on. One should, under such circumstances bear in mind that everything is predetermined and one cannot escape certain things in life. It is said that men of real wisdom are able to predict future happenings. That means the future is already set although we may not be aware of it. This understanding will make a person wise and guard himself against any negativity. Usually people get the feeling of acceptance to such happenings in life only after they undergo a lot of pain, hurt, disappointments and so on and after a long period of suffering they come to realize that they can do nothing to change the situation or happening and they come to terms with that. So it is said that 'time is the best healer'. Any negativity only leads to more and more negativity in one and the others. So even if one faces such happenings in life one should try to get over the feelings of negativity because generation of negativity in one harms that one as well as the others without bringing about any change for better of such situations. Since we know for certain that any negativity in whichever form it is bound to create unhappiness and misery for us and the others, we must determine to eliminate the negative tendencies up to our maximum capability. Then only there will be happiness and peace for one and all in this world".

"Swamiji, from what you say I understand that even if we get affected by the negativity of the others we should not react but we should respond in such a way that we do not return negativity for negativity. Suppose one's anger results in physical injury to the other who has been targeted then is it possible to remain calm and return positivity for such negativity. Is it possible practically? Kindly enlighten me about this".

"What I said is possible, but is never easy. Those who have elevated their minds spiritually, it is not at all difficult. There are a lot of anecdotes that show how the great saints and sages never bothered about any physical attack on them due to someone else's negativity. I do not know whether you know the story of sage *Jada Bharatha*, who was scolded, ridiculed and threatened of physical punishments by king *Rahugana* for not carrying his palanquin in a proper and steady manner. The king scolded sage *Bharatha* whom he took for an uncouth, dull headed mentally retarded muff and a fool, without knowing the real identity of the sage. He scolded the sage harshly with sarcastic words and told him that he will impose very harsh physical punishment to him for his carelessness in not carrying the palanquin in a steady manner. In return for his harsh and sarcastic comments the sage calmly looked up at the king who was sitting in the palanquin and said in a very calm voice, "Oh, king, you can impose any physical punishment upon me. You may also ridicule me. But I will never bother about these as I am not affected by your treatment of my body and mind because I am not the body or mind but the pure, imperishable soul that can never get hurt or destroyed." As soon as the king heard *Bharatha* speaking in this manner he at once realized that, that one must be a great soul and he got down from his palanquin and prostrated before the sage and pleaded for mercy for his ignorant acts. He then is said to have requested the sage to teach him *Atma Vidya* or the knowledge of one's self. The story relating to king *Vishvamitra* and Sage *Vasishta* also proves the point that the one who is mentally pure and powerful with positivity , though physically not very strong will be in a position to subjugate the one who projects negativity even if he is physically strong and is in command over a huge army that obeyed his commands. The huge army of king *Vishvamitra* ran helter shelter when Sage *Vasishta* who with his mental power finally bade the divine cow *Kamadenu* to drive away the king and his retinue who attacked sage *Vasishta* and his disciples in his Ashram. This happened several times and every time *Viswamitra* had to face defeat before the sage. It is then that the king realized that physical power and strength and possessions are nothing before one's mental power.

Even in our times the father of our nation Mahatma Gandhi had shown that it is possible. Whatever form of negativity he had to face during the freedom movement, he bore them patiently by adhering to the principle of non- violence. But such responses are possible only in the case of great souls. In the case of ordinary, worldly people, the best way to protect oneself physically and from negativity is to withdraw from such a situation. But if the other person on account of his ignorance or arrogance or the intensity of his emotion tries to inflict more and more physical harm continuously then, the affected person if he can, then may have to overpower the other one physically, without causing physical harm to that person so that he may refrain from inflicting physical pain to him. But such a reaction should come only after one tries and exhausts all possible ways to make the other person understand and refrain from such acts. However even if such situations become inevitable then one should act in such a manner that he never creates any hatred or vengeance against the other person and no thought residue remains in his memory about such acts because that will add to his accumulated tendencies or

Samskaras that he will have to carry to his subsequent births. Though this is difficult to practice one should try his level best whenever he comes across such situations in his life. When the *Kauravas* in an unrighteous manner continued to cause harm to the *Pandavas* Lord *Krishna* went as a mediator and tried all possible ways to bring about peace and establish a cordial relationship between the *Kauravas* and the *Pandavas*. It is only when he exhausted all ways and means and failed in avoiding the Great War at *Kurukshetra* that Lord Krishna bade *Arjuna* to do his duty as a prince and fight with the *Kauravas* for establishing Dharma or righteousness on earth".

"Sometimes we become negative and spread negativity around us. Why do such tendencies come up in us?"

"I have been stressing the fact that the negative tendencies in us affect ourselves as well as all the others around us. It also depletes our energy and that of those at whom we are projecting our negativity. But we always think that we are perfect. We never give sufficient thought to our own negative tendencies- their presence, and how much they affect others and their consequences on our own self. Once a person realizes that his own negative tendencies are bound to affect him more than the other person for whom it is intended, only then he will come to know how serious it is. When we allow negativity to sprout and grow in our mind then it will become like a ball that rolls along the ground collecting more and more dirt as it rolls. So negativity should never be encouraged in our mind. For that one should avoid seeing, hearing or speaking anything that causes negativity in oneself."

"One's own negative tendencies for example, hatred, jealousy, anger, arrogance, depression, self-pity, low self-esteem, inferiority complex, miserliness, narrow-mindedness, rudeness, etc. arise mainly due to egoistic tendencies that lead to expectations and uncontrolled desires in oneself that find ways and means to fulfill by comparing ourselves with the others. For example, we want others to praise us, appreciate us, admire us and agree with our opinions and views and so on. We also get negative feelings if any other person is more intelligent, more successful, more popular, more good looking, more healthy physically and mentally and successful in life and so on. Whenever one feels that the other person's views, thoughts, words or actions are not to his liking then also one tries to see all negative in him. All negative emotions and thoughts that we generate in our mind about some other person get expressed in words and deeds in a blunt, open manner or in a subtle, suggestive manner and this is the way of the world. A hypocrite who always smiles and talks politely may suppress his emotions only for a short time. Sooner or later all the pent up negative feelings will burst forth with double the speed and intensity."

"If others do not pay enough attention to us and ignore our presence when we are in a group and if some others are given more attention in that group then this creates negativity in us naturally without our own knowing and we wait for an opportunity to snub them or pay them in the same coin. Similarly when someone does not agree with our views or when somebody insults us we get angry. When we feel that somebody is more beautiful, more intelligent, smart, successful or prosperous in their life then we become jealous of them. Possessiveness and expectations, especially in the case of close and intimate relationships trigger negativity in oneself. For example when one feels that he or she has been cheated by his or her partner in life or his or her love and affection are being exploited then life becomes miserable to such a person and sometimes this leads to suicidal tendencies in one. If one has too much ambition and desires in his life and if he is unable to achieve at least a few of them then his unfulfilled desires also may generate negativity in him. When one's own children do not come up to one's expectations or when the grown up children do not reciprocate the love and affection and understand the sacrifices of their parents then the parents get dejected and depressed. When a person especially in the case of close relatives, friends, or neighbors etc. feels that the other person takes him for granted and any physical, mental, moral, or financial help that he extends to that person is not properly returned to him through affection or love or gratitude by the other person who receives them then such a feeling may also generate negativity in him and he may radiate negative energy".

"Swamiji, should we give importance to others' impressions about us in improving ourselves?"

"One should know that, how others view anyone is more often than not is highly subjective because it is based on their perception. It need not be unbiased or correct. So, one need not bother about the opinion of the others. To a certain extent one can give some weight to the opinion of others about oneself. If many consider a person as being negative to people and situations most of the time then, there must be some truth in that. Then that person must try to analyze his nature and try to rectify his negative tendencies for his own good as well as for the good of the others. But in the ultimate analysis one should know oneself. He should analyze his nature in an impartial, unbiased manner as a witness and then try to detect his negativities and drawbacks and then he should make a very sincere and honest effort to rectify the negativity in him and make himself and the others happy and peaceful. If one can do that then he can make his own life a grand celebration"

"It is also true that one will not know how he looks unless he sees his own reflection in a mirror. The mirror if it is a good one will reflect the image of a person's face correctly. On the other hand a bad mirror can only give a distorted image of the person who looks at the mirror. Similar is the case with other's opinion or judgment about us as well. Only people who can view the others in an impartial and unbiased manner can view another's tendencies and can assess the person properly. On the other hand the one who is biased, who is waiting for an opportunity to degrade the other person because he does not like him or because he is not being appreciated by the other one for all his views, words and actions will only at the very first opportunity condemn the other person saying that he is full of negativity. Sometimes in the case of intimate relationships like husband and wife the views of one about the other may be highly boosting to the other or damaging. If they love each other intensely and are loyal and affectionate to each other then no negativity will be detected by either of the two in the other. On the other hand in the absence of love, loyalty and affection each will only try to find fault and point out the defects in the other always. So in such cases it is better that one tries to know his virtues as well as the vices through self-analysis and then wipe out the negativity or the vices with those of virtues or positive attitude or feelings. It is also possible that when we give importance to other's view about ourselves then, there is every chance that someone who has a very low impression about us is able to create a very low level of confidence in ourselves. This will make us depressed, and fill us with self-pity and so on and ultimately this diffidence will make `us good for nothing. So one should always try to understand oneself in an impartial manner through self-analysis and do all that are necessary to improve himself so that he can lead a happy and peaceful life and also help others in making their life the best possible."

"Many feel that the negativity in them is caused by others and by situations. What do you say for that Swamiji"?

"There are people who strongly believe that any kind of negativity in them is because of others who project negativity at them and also because of the situations that are negative to them. These are the people who have a high esteem of themselves and they deliberately try to cover up their negativity by throwing blame on the others or on situations. These people think that they are forced to become negative because others project negativity at them or because situations force them to become negative. But one should know that only when people react to what they consider as negative either in the others or in the situations the negative tendencies come up in one's mind. But if they are able to see positivity in these or ignore the negativity, or respond to these in a proper manner then there is no need for them to become negative".

"Sometimes we create and project negativity in return for negativity- for example some harsh words from someone else make us retort in the same way negatively. But why should this happen even after knowing that negativity results in harm to all?"

"No doubt when we release our negative energy in the form of thoughts or words or deeds we may get some immediate relief because the negative energy in us gets dissipated or released and we calm down and also because such actions will boost our ego. But the negative feeling cannot go away by such acts. After some time it is bound to come back again. It is only ignorance that makes them return negativity for negativity."

"*When one suppresses his negativity, does it harm him*"?

"Any suppression or controlling uses up more energy and it robs the body of the energy that otherwise could have been used for maintaining a better physical and mental health. The negative emotions strain the body by taxing the adrenal glands and in the process it uses up the nutrients that are otherwise used by the body for sustaining itself. This results in fatigue and lowered levels of vitality and vigor. Suppression of emotions also create more and more negative feelings like frustration, anger, physical pain, depression, hatred, self-pity and therefore it is suicidal. When we suppress any negative emotion at any time then it is bound to bounce back with double force in the most unexpected manner at the most unexpected time. So the solution lies in awareness of the problem and finding out ways or means to tackle them in the best possible manner in a positive way. The study of impact of emotions on our physical and mental health has given rise to the emergence of a new field of medicine in modern times that is called the energy Psychology".

"*Are our emotional acts that come out spontaneously from us always bad, Swamiji?*"

"Sometimes we think, feel, say or do something negatively in an impulsive and also in an emotional manner and then regret about it later. We must know that when we are impulsive our emotions dominate us. Strong emotions block clear, unbiased and proper thinking. At such times the intelligence is bypassed. So before any negative thought enters in to our mind that gives rise to negative words and actions, we should observe our attitude and thoughts and the emotions that dominate us and that would give rise to negative words or actions. Spontaneous actions are good in the case of positive emotions only. Emotions that lead to spontaneous acts of love, kindness, sacrifice etc. are good, valuable as well as important in one's life. They also motivate us. But whenever anyone gets any negative emotions like hatred, anger etc. then it is better to allow such emotions to cool down. So while it is better to allow the heart to dominate in the case of positive feelings we must allow unbiased reasoning to dominate in the case of our negative emotions. It is better to refrain ourselves from acting or reacting quickly under such circumstances. Instead, we should analyze the cause of such negative emotions silently. We should not be carried away by the impulsive mood. We must try to view it in an unbiased manner, as a witness without involving or entangling ourselves in that. We should take enough time to calm down and to feel relaxed because only a calm and relaxed mind can be reasonable and rational and can view things in an objective and impartial manner. We should also think of the consequences of the negative feelings and analyze whether such impulsive mood is beneficial to the physical and the mental well-being of ourselves and of all those around us. If we can practise this then we will realize that not only that we are able to cool down and allow our emotions to pass with a let go attitude but we can also see that the negative emotions run out of its energy up to the last so that, we can get over such negative energy and even change such attitude into positive ones. We must know that the one who is slow to any negative emotion and the one who has conquered his negative emotions is more powerful than the mighty one who is able to capture a vast kingdom. It is said that whenever you get any negative feeling you should postpone its use to a later time and it is found that when you do so, you may not bother to harm anybody with your negativity afterwards, that is, after sometime".

"*How to prevent negativity arising in our mind as they are actually our own making*"?

"The negative energy gets generated in ourselves by our own negative thoughts, feelings and emotions. It is our own making. None other than oneself is responsible for such a state of mind. Whenever we get negative emotions then, immediately we must find out the source of that negativity and then instead of brooding over the source we have to focus on the solutions for the problem. We must also train our mind in such a way that we have less and less negativity over a period of time and also as we grow older and that is the path of wisdom. We must also make an honest assessment of our own nature and character, understand our own negative thoughts and find out why such negative thoughts are coming up in our mind, what are its consequences? After knowing the answers for these questions we must make an effort to gradually minimize them by disciplining our mind and also inculcating positive tendencies in our mind".

"We must also understand that nothing is permanent in this world nor will it be the same forever whether it is our life itself, or relationships, our possessions, success or failure and so on. So it is better not to get entangled in all these. We have to perform our duties to the best of our ability, in the best possible manner, as per our role in life as a parent, husband, wife, child, friend, and neighbor, co-worker, as a social being and as a citizen and so on without any expectation. This understanding will reduce the bad or negative tendencies in us to a great extent".

"Whenever any negative thoughts arise in our mind we must be conscious enough to catch them as soon as they appear in our mind and remove such negativity even in the beginning stages itself by repeated thinking that it is not good for anyone".

"Sometimes problems and difficulties are blown out of proportions even though they are actually minor problems that can be solved easily with some effort. This also creates negativity like fear, anxiety or tension in one. The best way to get out of such negativity is to remain cool and confident, and after analyzing the problem find solutions by one's own effort or with the help of others. The negative emotions only will make the mind get perturbed and upset and such a mind loses all its strength and its power in finding a solution to any problem that one faces in life".

"One should also not allow oneself to brood over his past negativity. It will help neither himself nor the others. We have to think and ponder over our past negative emotions so that we learn from them and improve ourselves by correcting our behavior so that we do not repeat such negative thoughts, feelings, words or acts. We should as far as possible do our might to improve ourselves so that it will benefit ourselves and the others around us."

"Another way to minimize our negativity is to be calm and silent. Negativity sometimes arises because of unnecessary talk and gossip. So one should as far as possible avoid too much of talk because there is a possibility that the more you talk the more you will be misunderstood or you affect the other person's feelings thereby creating negative energy in both ourselves as well the others with whom we are talking."

"However, all the negativities in us cannot be eliminated completely or all on a sudden or even at the same time. The first step is to become aware of the fact that we have negative thoughts that get expressed in words and through actions. This knowledge may be only theoretical at this stage. In spite of this knowledge a person may continue to have more and more negativity in him or he may ignore it or may not take any effort to tackle it in the best possible way. The second stage is to become aware of each of the negative feelings, words and acts as soon as they rise in the mind and expressed outwardly through words and actions and at this stage one repents for each of such negativity with the knowledge that any type of negativity harms the one who projects it before it harms the other person on whom it is projected. In the third stage not only that one comes to know of his drawback, and repents for that, but more importantly he makes a resolve not to repeat them in future. The fourth stage is to make his mind understand about the evil consequences of negativity anywhere or in any one and with this knowledge minimize such thoughts, words and acts up to his maximum capacity by nipping them in the bud stage itself and generate as much positivity as possible and follow this constantly in his life."

"After all there is nothing in this world that is totally negative. No one is totally bad or totally good. Man is a mixture of both these qualities. So each one of us have a share of both good and bad positive and negative. The only difference is that a good man has more positivity in him while a bad person has more of negativity in him. But it is necessary that we should try to avoid and eliminate negativity as far as possible in ourselves and safeguard ourselves from creating negativity on account of other's behavior or because of the situations or because of our own weaknesses. This is ultimately possible only by changing ourselves for better that is by self-improvement".

"One has to remember always that negativity in any one will undoubtedly make that person unhappy and restless. He can enjoy no peace and no happiness because of that. That means eradicating negativity with positivity through persistent efforts of self-analysis is the only ultimate way for a happy and peaceful living. No doubt it is a very difficult task. But this is the only way to enjoy a good physical and mental health and thereby the best possible life."

4
Positivity

"Swamiij, you said negativity that ruins a man can be removed ultimately by creating and strengthening positivity in us. Actually what is meant by positivity"?

"Positivity simply means good conduct and righteousness that we usually call as virtues of life. It is the goodness and the righteousness in one that overcomes any evil with good, falsehood with truth, hatred with love and compassion, miserliness with broadmindedness and charity, pessimism with optimism, criticism with appreciation, and intolerance with tolerance and so on. It is a tendency towards self-improvement. According to Descartes virtues consist in correct reasoning that should guide our actions. When you create any positive thought it will automatically grow in you and will bring about many more positive qualities. It is like the planting of a seed that will give rise to many seeds later on through the fruits of the tree of that particular seed that you have sown. Once you sow a seed sufficiently deep in to the soil then in due course it will sprout in to a seedling provided you pay attention to it; that means if you water the soil. You need not do anything more than that. Then at the appropriate time you will see the seedling coming out of the earth. It is automatic. Similarly, once you plant the seed of any good or positive thought and nurture it in your mind then it is bound to come out in positive words and deeds that will bring happiness for one and all. But just as one positive thought generates more and more positive thoughts one single negative thought will also generate more and more negative thoughts that will result in unhappiness and misery for one and all so, one must be careful to generate only virtuous, positive thoughts in his mind".

"Swamiji, what is the importance of positivity?"

"*Mahatma Gandhi* said "keep your thoughts positive because your thoughts become your words. Keep your words positive because your words become your behavior. Keep your behavior positive because your behavior becomes your habits. Keep your habits positive because your habits become your values. Keep your values positive because your values become your destiny".

"All religions of the world and spirituality since ancient times have stressed the need for positivity. Virtues that are good and that bring happiness and fulfillment to oneself and to the others can be termed as positive and they fill with positivity in oneself. They indicate the moral excellence in one. It is the positive trait or quality that is morally good and this is the foundation of a good human being. Positive thinking, positive words and positive actions enhance the individual wellbeing and also the collective well-being. Every religion stresses virtues and good conduct as essential to man. When positivity is 100% without any adulteration then it becomes purity. For example if love that is one important quality of positivity is hundred percent unconditional and unselfish then it becomes pure. But selfish love is adulterated and it can never be totally pure".

"Just as weeds grow in plenty and on its own accord in a barren land that is not used to its capacity properly, the mind also that is not put to use properly for positive thinking will become the fertile soil for all types of negativity and as the saying goes it will become a "devil's work shop." On the other hand a man who practices virtues will be rewarded with peace of mind and happiness and he makes his life worthy and also purposeful for him as well as for the others".

"How can we generate positivity in us, Swamiji?"

"First of all we must have the conviction that all virtues that lead to positivity are godly and divine because you do good because of the prompting of your inner voice where the divinity resides and the inner voice or the conscience will always guide you in the right direction. When you are able to understand the divinity in you, you cannot do anything but good to all. It is the devil in you that makes you negative and become bad. We must try to awaken the divinity in us. If we want to make our life happy and peaceful then we should drive away the devil of negativity as soon as it enters into our mind and fill that place immediately with positivity. When we remember, express and practice positive feelings always then this will drive away the negativity in us automatically. But then as *George Eliot* has said, it will never rain roses. When we want to have more roses, then we must plant more roses. So also is the case with virtues or positivity".

"There is no use in seeking happiness from outside, from others or from situations as happiness and peace is inside us; it is a state of mind and you can achieve it only by your own effort. Both negativity as well as positivity are nothing but opposite states of mind. When we perceive any one or any situation as bad or negative then we generate all negative and bad qualities in us thinking that it is only natural and only thereby we can get solace. But then it is nothing but ignorance. Both negativity as well as positivity must be returned with positivity. When one can do this always then he becomes the divine, God, the Almighty. It is the law of nature that when we give the world our best then best will come back to us. Positivity or negativity is a feeling or thought in the mind that comes out as words or actions. So if we can tackle our thoughts, emotions or feelings then the words and actions can be tackled in an effortless manner. We must try to see positivity in each and every person and in each and every situation. It is possible through positive outlook and perception. When we make the life of others happy through our virtues then the others will be induced to make our life happier".

"Merely thinking about positivity and its values, importance and benefits one cannot create positivity in himself. This needs an all-out effort so that one can start generating at least a few virtues or positivity and he will be surprised to see that more and more positivity gets generated in his mind automatically. We have to create them, make use of them every moment of our life. We must fuel ourselves with positivity just as flame is made more powerful and extensive by fuelling it."

"As human beings it is our responsibility to generate positivity in ourselves so that it brings happiness and peace not only for ourselves but also on whom the positivity is radiated or projected by us. It also spreads positive energy around us just as negativity spreads negative energy all around us. It is also a fact that a few positive qualities in one will attract more and more positive values in him because he comes to realize the good effects of positive behavior. Even if one is unable to know the benefits of his positivity, it is bound to generate more and more similar virtues automatically resulting in more and more positive energy in that person".

"Swamiji, I now understand that when we send positive energy to others through our positivity then both we and the others are benefited. Are the Karmas or the rituals performed for the dead got anything to do with positivity?"

"As human beings it is also our duty to send positive vibrations to those departed souls who are no more with us and who are dead and gone. Mere brooding over their death and grieve for them intensely will not serve any purpose. Such acts will only generate negativity and hence the negative vibrations in the mind of the mourner and also in the dead because the unhappiness of those who are left behind will only create unhappiness for the departed soul and the resultant negative tendency in its mind is likely to add to its already *Samskaras* or past accumulated tendencies that would affect the dead one's subsequent birth. That will definitely weaken the dead and the departed one may become helpless because neither can he make himself visible nor can he contact and communicate with his near and dear ones who mourn for the loss because he is no longer in his physical form or body. When one is dead his physical body is destroyed either by burning or burying the dead body. That means that body gets disintegrated and mixes with the five elements of nature. But with death the mind does not perish. The mind in the form of thoughts that got converted into tendencies, after sometime will enter into a new body and it will enjoy or suffer the consequences of its positive or negative qualities of the earlier births. So the only way by which we can help the dead is to send positive thoughts and vibrations to them so that they will be charged with the necessary positive vibrations from their near and dear ones. The positive vibrations will help them to drive away their negative tendencies. We know that negativity causes great harm and misery not only to the one who has it but also for the others. Even after one's death the accumulated negative tendencies of one's mind may reach the persons on whom they are targeted making them suffer. So the *Karmas* performed for such a dead person will help the dead one to acquire more and more positivity and that would eliminate his negativity. Actually all the rituals that are called as *Karmas* and prayers and *Poojas* or worship for the dead with all the things which they had a liking when they were in their physical body are meant only for such results, to help them as well as the others who are alive. These rituals also give a sense of satisfaction to the doer of the rituals that he has done his best to help the departed soul as this is the only thing that he can do for the departed soul. After a certain period of time the departed one may enter into a new body and all the memories of its past birth might be erased from the conscious mind and it may not know anything about the *Karmas* or rituals performed for its sake. But even then the positive vibrations as a result of the fond memories and the positive vibrations on account of prayers and the rituals and so on may probably reach that one who is in the new body in an unconscious manner even though the memories of the past are erased from the conscious mind of that one who is in a new body and that one may benefit out of the positive vibrations sent towards it. Although these things cannot be proved as none has actually experienced it still this is what the great elevated souls have been telling us always. But mere mechanical and outward performance of rituals will serve no purpose. If the intention in performing such rituals for the dead is to radiate positive vibrations to them and make them happy and be peaceful then the rituals and prayers are to be performed in a very honest and sincere mind and with full faith in them. Otherwise it will only become a mere mockery of such belief systems as such acts will not serve any purpose."

"Swamiji, my father one day during his last days called me and asked me to sit by his side and told me that after his death it is not at all necessary for me to perform any Karmas for him and instead he told me that if at all I can,

then it will be more than enough if I can feed a few poor people with simple food instead of performing all the elaborate Karmas as per our tradition and taking his ashes to sacred rivers or the sea for immersion and so on after his death. I did as per his wishes and did the poor feeding to as many poor people as I could. Do you think that was sufficient?"

"Undoubtedly, in my view your father directed you to do the best thing that you could have done as a human being, especially in modern times when there are many poor people who lead their life by filling only half of their stomach. Giving food to the needy is one of the greatest virtues of life. Definitely this act on your part, I am sure, would have sent a lot of positive vibrations to your father after his death".

"Swamiji, kindly explain to me the benefits of Positivity".

"While negativity damages one's physical and mental health, positivity always strengthens one's mental and physical well-being. It is said that positive qualities that lead to positive thinking cures even fatal diseases. Simultaneously it brings calmness and purity to the mind. This results in clarity of vision. A calm and pure mind enhances the spiritual well-being of a person by transforming and elevating his mind. All positive virtues contribute towards all these even without our own knowing".

"No doubt, in the day to day life of ordinary worldly persons negativity cannot be totally eliminated. However we must always see that our mind is filled with more and more positive emotions and thoughts and feelings and less of negative emotions, thoughts and feelings that result in either positive or negative words and actions. Positivity always generates positive energy in one where as negativity results in negative energy. All happiness and peace that any human beings craves for in his life can be obtained only by positivity whereas negativity destroys all happiness and peace in one's life and also makes one's life miserable, unhappy and without peace of mind."

"Researchers are of the opinion that the benefits of positivity occurs when the ratio of positive to negative emotions is at least 3 to 1. So, as far as possible we must create and strengthen as many positive qualities as possible in us for enjoying our life to the brim.

We must make an honest effort to counteract and mitigate the negative tendencies that can be termed as the vices in us by maximizing those virtues that are positive. At the end of each day, before going to bed we must make a list of all positive thoughts and emotions that we had that day and also all the negative feelings that we entertained that day and examine how many negative thoughts we were able to detect and get over and how many positive thoughts we were able to strengthen that day. After knowing that we must try to reduce the negative thoughts and enhance the number of positive thoughts each day because one can lead a life of happiness, peace and fulfillment and enjoy his life to the maximum only by enhancing positivity to the maximum and by reducing negativity to the minimum level.

When one is able to generate and project more positivity it also results in more positivity in the other on account of the positive vibrations that reach him and in this manner the whole world can be filled with positive energy that makes everyone's life blissful. More and more positivity in one also will make one more lovable and more successful in life and so on. Such a person will become a role model for all the others and this would make his life more purposeful and worthy".

"Swamiji, how does positivity in one help him in removing his negativity?"

"Positivity is light and Negativity is darkness. Just as darkness cannot be removed by darkness or by any other except light similarly only positivity can remove negativity in us. If the windows in a room are closed during the day time and if we complain that the room is dark then it is not going to make the room bright. Only when we open the windows and let the sun shine enter into the room, the room will be lit. Similarly by merely recognizing the negativity in us will not result in any solution because as darkness can be removed only by letting in the sunshine in to the room similarly negativity also can be eliminated by letting in and strengthening the positive qualities and virtues in us. Once the positive tendencies enter into our mind then automatically the negative emotions in us will disappear without any effort on our part. We should never try to suppress or control our negative feelings and emotions because they are harmful and will not serve the purpose that is their removal. Just as we have prevented the sunshine that gives brightness to the room we also prevent or at least do not make any effort to bring up and utilize the positivity in us. Even though man is a mixture of both positive and negative tendencies, we know that only positivity can make our life blissful. So we have to strengthen the positivity in us so that the negative in us will disappear on its own accord. We have to attract as much positive energy as possible to dispel as much negative energy as possible to reach our goal of peace and happiness through best possible life."

"*What are positive and negative energies*"?

"Actually energy is neutral; it is neither positive nor negative. Thoughts are energy. This energy gets radiated through an electromagnetic energy field that connects all matter in this universe. It has also been found both in science as well as in spirituality that all matter is only energy condensed to a low vibration and every being in it is a part of this same energy. The ancient Indian *Rishis* of the past pointed out that the universe itself is a bundle of great energy. This energy can be channeled inwards creating a sense of wellbeing or misery in one. If we create negative energy in us then we create untold miseries for us as well as for the others. On the contrary, if we are able to make use of the energy in a positive way then it results unimaginable peace and happiness not only for ourselves but also for the others. It is the tendencies, emotions or thoughts that make the energy either positive or negative. Positive thoughts convert one's energy into positive energy; so also negative thoughts generate negative energy in one. Positive energy empowers us and strengthens us; whereas negative energy depletes our energy there by make us weak. When there is more positive energy in one it becomes easy for him to drive away the negative energy that he has and it also results in more and more positive energy that results in more and more happiness and peace. When we are full of negative energy life is miserable and unhappy and we experience lack of peace and tranquility in our mind. But with positive emotions and thoughts our energy becomes positive and our life becomes the most interesting and blissful. Positive energy makes us healthy, energetic, and inspired and so on and these result in peace and happiness to us. On the contrary the negative energy that gives rise to negative vibrations make our life miserable, exhausted, sad, desperate, disinterested etc. and make our life the most unhappy and with no peace of mind. Positive energy that is radiated will bring back positive energy and negative energy that is sent out will bring back negative energy."

"What is the importance of maximizing positivity?"

"To fill ourselves with positivity is not an easy task but it is not impossible either. One must know that the road to positivity is the best but is also the roughest and steepest in this world. But if one really wants to be happy, loved, appreciated, admired by others and be successful and if one wants to make his life happy, peaceful, worthy, purposeful and fulfilling then it is the only way. Even if one cannot fill one's mind completely with positive thoughts at least he can strive for generating more and more positivity each day.

The difficulty is many of us do not give importance to the lasting benefits of the virtues that are necessary in one's life for realizing the best possible life. We give importance only to the short term results but not the long term benefits. We ignore the fact that any negative behavior or thought can lead to temporary emotional satisfaction cannot last for long. For example when a person contradicts our point of view then we easily get irritated, angry, and immediately we try to snub the other person thinking in an ignorant manner that we have made a point over the other and established our superior intellect or knowledge. We are forgetting the fact that our gain is less when compared to our loss and the gain also is temporary. It might have boosted our ego but then at what cost? Because in the process we lose a great deal as we are bound to lose a friendly person. This also fills our mind as well of the other with negativity because no longer the relationship between the two can be as before and cordial. On the other hand if we try to detect the points that are agreeable to both and have a talk about this then it will satisfy the other person and it will also not create any negative feeling to both. We may not be in agreement with the other person fully. But why can't we ignore and be silent about those points where there is disagreement? We need not be hypocritical and praise the other in a false manner. This will make the good relationships to be cordial and sincere as before by creating positivity in both. Similar is the case with any positive thought or emotion, word or deed".

"How can one think, feel and act positively?"

"To think, feel, speak, and do positively one should cultivate humility instead of pampering his ego, should be thoughtful of the feelings of the others, must be cooperative, must be broadminded, friendly, kind, sympathetic, compassionate, have sincere and pure love, be accommodative, be without expectation of any reward for his positivity and he must also know that he has to restrict his worldly desires as far as possible. This is because one's sense of ego, that leads to attachments and expectations and too much of desires in the mind of one become the hurdles in generating and projecting as much positivity as possible for him. One should also be a good person basically at the level of his thoughts because any positive thought gives rise to positive feeling, words and actions while any negative thought gives rise to negative feeling, words and actions. Positive thinking is that thought that creates and concentrates on the good in oneself and that of the others in an equal manner. Positive people are always good natured, with many, if not all of the good qualities of life because they have a favorable disposition towards one and all".

"All positive virtues are to be practiced without any expectation of any return of any kind, whether it is love, kindness, forgiveness, empathy, compassion etc. We should be lavish in acquiring the virtues and in spending it on others. *Swami Vivekananda* once said, "In the world take always the position of the giver; help, give service, give any little thing you can but keep out of barter. Make no condition and none will be imposed. Let us give out of our own bounty, just as God gives to us".

"We should be like nature that gives even without asking. Nature does not discriminate anything. For example a tree does not provide shade or fruits, after discriminating whether one deserves the shade or fruit. It just gives. That is its very nature. It also does not expect anything in return from the one who is provided with its shade or fruit and so on. When a person is able to be like nature in giving and projecting his positive nature, with no expectation of anything in return and without discriminating then he becomes a great *Mahatma*, a great soul and anything they think and utter becomes true and it happens. Ancient scriptures teach us to see everything as God or as ourselves and use everything in this world with the thought that everything belongs to God although we are allowed to make use of all that the God has blessed us with in this world. They also teach us to view the others as ourselves or even as Gods. If we are able to keep these teachings in our mind always and think, speak and act accordingly then, we can never project negativity towards any one. When we view everything as God, our creator, then we get only positive feelings like love, respect, etc. towards all. When we view that everything belongs to God only and we are here only to make use of all things provided by God and not to possess or own it then we will not become selfish as the thought of possessing anything will never arise in our mind".

"Swamiji, you said that we should be like nature in projecting positivity. But is it really possible to be like that? Because in today's world sometimes we feel cheated by the other for whom we did something good. I remember one experience in my own life in this".

"Tell me your experience then. Let me also know about it. Go on". Said the *Swamiji* and I began to narrate that incident.

"It happened when I was in my 20s. As usual I was very busy with my usual routine household works and with cooking in the morning after my bath. As I usually got ready for the college only after finishing all my work I was not well dressed and my hair was also not kept in order. It is then that my husband called me and said, "Look, some girl is standing outside. She wants to meet you". When I went out I saw a little girl around nine to ten years of age. She was crying and when I asked her the reason she told me that she has no parents and she lives with some close relatives of hers who are looking after all her needs since she lost her parents a few months back. That morning they brought her to *Tirupathi* and after asking her to wait in a certain place in the bus stand and telling her that they will be back soon they went away never to return. Now she is left alone in this new place where she has no body to help her. She has no money with her to return to her place that is a close by village. It was already 9'o clock in the morning and I had to get ready to go to the college. Somehow I felt that I should help her in some way so I asked her whether she had anything to eat. She said she did not have anything since that morning. So I gave her breakfast and gave her some money and asked her to go to the bus stand and get into the bus for her place the name of which she knew and she went away after wiping her tears. For some moments I stood there looking at that small girl. Poor child I thought. Then I came back and got ready and went to my college. That evening while I was returning from the college I noticed the same girl standing near the college gate telling the same story to everyone who was passing that way. I went near her and asked her "I remember you coming to me this morning with the same story. I even offered you money and breakfast. Why didn't you return to your place?" The girl quickly turned her back towards me and ran away. And I felt really cheated. Such incidents will make anyone lose the qualities of sympathy or charity for example, *Swamiji*".

"O K, It is natural for you to have got such a feeling. But although you could view things in the morning objectively, you failed to do so in the evening when you saw the child repeating the same story. At once you came to the conclusion that the child has made that as her profession. But do you know there are very many children who are threatened and forced to beg by creating such stories. They are also trapped and they are unable to come out and escape. If that has been the case with this child also would you ever blame the child? You will only pity that child all the more. That means before coming to any conclusion, especially if it is a negative one we should try to view objectively".

"Now, as far your doubt as to how one can be like nature in making oneself always useful to the others. Look, as I told you already a tree does not discriminate anything or anybody. It will not say that it will give its leaves, flowers and fruits and also shade and so on for those whom it considers as worthy. Irrespective of the fact whether a person is good or bad, praises it or condemns it, whether it is a man or a woman or a child, it gives everything that it can without expecting anything in return. Even to the one who cuts its braches it serves as firewood. The tree also does not compare its capacity to yield flowers or fruits and so on with any other tree. Some trees yield more and some yield less. Whatever it can it gives unmindful of what the other trees are giving. But that does not mean that it can be exploited. If we ask any tree to yield more or less fruits, flowers and leaves then it will not. It will also not yield fruits and flowers during offseason even if you ask it or threaten it. If you nourish it more it will yield more but if you do not maintain it properly and still if you want it to yield more it will not. Anything in nature behaves like this only. But nature will allow man to exploit her up to a limit. Beyond that it will start reacting and man will be unable to withstand its fury. This is the natural law. For example deforestation has resulted in water scarcity everywhere because of lack of rains and proper and timely rains can be there only when we do not destroy the forests and trees. So like nature why can't man also contribute his might for the good of others? Like nature man should also project positivity to all without any discrimination, without expectation, without concern for praise or criticism and without comparing himself with that of another. Like nature man can also allow others to exploit him up to a limit. But beyond that limit he can withdraw himself totally from people who project negativity and situations that are harmful to him so that he does not forego his positivity that is valuable not only to him but also for the others.

We have to go on projecting as many positive qualities as possible till our last breath. Why can't we take the role of a giver who gives all that he can without expectations instead of playing the role of a taker or a beggar? Why can't we be broadminded, magnanimous and royal by giving instead of begging others for love, affection, kindness, sympathy, compassion, and so on and so forth? Once we decide and become the one who gives but not receives then surely we can hold our head high and it will make our life purposeful and worthy and will pave the way for happiness and peace for one and all."

"Now I understand Swamiji. Kindly tell me about the impact of positivity on our day to day life"?

"Positivity found in any one contributes towards the physical, mental and spiritual well-being of that person. It is our day to day experience that whenever we feel good we always feel strong, less stressed, healthy, happy and peaceful. Positivity helps us to face and solve the challenges and difficulties of life in a better way. Those who are positive with virtues use the power of their mind in a positive manner and they remain calm and composed, relaxed and they also enjoy their life to the brim. We must know that we have the potential and power to change the way we want, think, and feel. So why not make ourselves think and feel positively and reap all its benefits for a sound body- mind well- being for ourselves as well as for the others around us and enjoy our life by making it purposeful, worthy, Peaceful and Happy?"

"Swamiji kindly explain to me about some of the important virtues that one should practice in his life to achieve the best possible life".

"All positive qualities, or virtues or thoughts or feelings or emotions contribute towards positivity in one. These are innumerable in number and every one of us knows about these virtues as these feelings arise in the mind through rational thinking or in the heart through emotions. A few of these are, Compassion, cheerfulness, caring, love, accountability, appreciation, fairness, forgiveness, fortitude, generosity, gentleness, gratitude, helpfulness, honesty, humility, integrity, joyfulness, kindness, magnanimity, modesty, openness, patience, perseverance, persistence, piety, prudence, reliability, respect, righteousness, selflessness, sympathy, empathy, sensitivity, objectivity, simplicity, sincerity, tactfulness, tolerance, trustworthiness, courage, optimism, politeness, courtesy, self-control, thoughtfulness, forbearance, self-esteem, equanimity, patience and so on.

Sri Krishna lists out a few positive qualities possessed by those whom He categorizes as born in divine state. These are fearlessness, purity of heart, steadfastness in action, knowledge, alms-giving, control of senses, sacrifice, study of scriptures, austerity, straight forwardness, harmlessness, truth, absence of anger, renunciation, peacefulness, absence of crookedness, compassion, gentleness, modesty, absence of fickle mindedness, vigor, forgiveness, fortitude, purity of thought, word and deed, absence of hatred, absence of pride etc. These virtues will result in a very cordial and a harmonious society where there will not be any negativity like ill feeling, hatred, jealousy and so on. Under such circumstances the whole life will become a benediction for one and all. Each will get the best from life by giving out the best in him.

Some of the virtues strengthen one's character in a positive way and become beneficial to the one who possesses it in a direct manner. These same qualities indirectly benefit the others around him as well because they help the possessor of such qualities in generating positive qualities or virtues in others that benefit others also along with him. For example if a person has the virtue of joyfulness, or optimism then it will help him to overcome the negativity projected at him by others or by situations that are perceived and therefore considered as adverse to him. He will be in a position to tackle these calmly. This is the direct benefit of such a virtue that benefits the possessor directly. At the same time these qualities also will enhance his power of acceptability and tolerance and so on in him that he has to project towards others for their happiness resulting in creation of positive qualities in them as well. There are a few positive feelings that are to be expressed through words and acts like love, sympathy, empathy, compassion, kindness, forgiveness, charity and so on. These benefit the sender and the recipient of such thoughts directly and in a positive manner. For example if a person forgives another for the hurt that the other person has caused, then it will make the one who has forgiven noble and it will also make the other person who caused the mental injury to feel very bad and he will only try to emulate the other person who has forgiven him whenever any harm is done to him by some other in some other situation. That means the positive quality in one has benefited him as well as the other person directly and simultaneously and if this process goes on in all similar cases where any negativity is returned with positivity then the whole world will become a paradise on earth".

"Swamiji, kindly tell me something more about virtues, at least some of these virtues that you have listed out."

"All virtues are important and should be followed if one wants the best possible life for himself and for the others. Which are those virtues about which you want me to say something?"

As I did not know what to ask him I became silent. Seeing my plight the *Swamiji* continued. *"All right, let me tell you briefly about some of the virtues"*.

Honesty and Truthfulness

"The virtue of honesty and truthfulness is related to integrity and straight forwardness. In honesty there is harmony in thought, word and deed. It is being truthful, genuine, and trustworthy with no falsehood whatsoever. Honesty comes from purity of thought, word and deed. *Albert Einstein* stated that "Whoever is careless with truth in small matters cannot be trusted with important matters". "Truth lightens our burdens. It lights up our pathway with the radiance of joy" said Anonymous.

When one's heart really opens up one cannot and will not utter lies. That is the truth of truth. No doubt truth is harder to speak and flattery or untruth may be easier to speak. But even then we should choose to speak truth and truth only- nothing else except truth and that is the mark of a great soul. When we utter lies we cover up so many facts and give so many explanations that become very difficult for us to remember and it becomes a heavy burden to us. But truth is only one and needs no memory. The one who utters truth always feels light at heart. Also truth cannot be crushed or buried as it will rise again. But that does not mean that one should hurt the others by saying that he is open-minded and frank. It is said that honesty is the best policy. It may sound simple but is very difficult to practise at all times with all people. The ancient Indian scriptures say that truth is to be told in such a manner that it does not hurt the feelings of the other person. That means it must be told in a smooth, gentle, and in a polite manner. The truth when uttered also should not be interpreted as criticisms or lack of support or flattery and in case it brings about dire consequences then it is better to be silent about such truths. When the utterance of truth gives rise to good feelings in others then one must be broadminded and lavish enough in expressing it."

Contentment

Contentment is the feeling of wanting or desiring no more than what one has around himself, whether they are people, objects or circumstances or situations. This does not however mean contentment in one's physical and mental efforts to become happy and peaceful in life and in imbibing all that result in good for others. It only refers to desire for the material, worldly things. Less desire will lead to contentment whereas more and more desires will lead to discontentment. It also leads to tension, anxiety, stress etc. in maintaining what one has already achieved materially in one's life. The one who is contented will have more mental stability, clarity, peace and happiness for himself and he will also be in a position to pass on these to all the others as well".

Joyfulness

Joyfulness is a feeling of joy. Those who are joyful experience cheerfulness, happiness, peace, love, a sense of well-being and they are enthusiastic in everything that they do. It is said joyfulness is the infallible sign of the presence of God in man. "A joyful heart is the normal result of a heart burning with love" says *Mother Teresa.* Joy and happiness are inseparable twins. They cannot be separated. It is also contagious. One who possesses this virtue is in a position to pass it on to the others even without one's own knowing.

Happiness and joy comes not because there are no problems in life but because of the ability to face and find solutions for such problems and challenges. We must also try to enjoy our life without comparing ourselves with others. It is said that joy and happiness together is like a perfume; you cannot pour it on others unless you have a drop of it in yourself. It is like a single lamp that can light innumerable lamps. Those who are joyful are always at peace because these two qualities make one calm and at peace with in himself because he does not experience any inner turmoil due to conflicts of interests. This is because when one is peaceful then he becomes relaxed and this makes his brain work properly and he takes correct decisions at the correct moments. The peace that one enjoys internally also makes him tolerant, understanding etc. with everything and in every situation. We must also understand that happiness from material objects that satisfy our wants and desires can give only temporary happiness because as soon as one want or desire is satisfied another one will take its place. That means it is not real happiness because after some time they may create unhappiness also as one gets many negative feelings that are associated with the protection and maintenance of those objects that he is able to possess. The real joy comes from the feeling good, saying good and doing good for others".

Modesty and Humbleness

"Modesty is the propriety or decency in speech and behavior. It is freedom from vanity and boastfulness. The person who is modest will exhibit moderate estimation of his talents, capabilities and importance. He will be simple and free from egotism. Modesty is the gentle art of enhancing one's charm. However modesty should be devoid of hypocrisy as false modesty or false humility is worse than arrogance."

"Humbleness or humility is one of the greatest virtues of the one who has conquered his own mind. One who is modest will also have humility and vice versa. One who possesses this virtue can easily conquer egoism that is the root cause of negativity in this world. A humble person is without pride or boasting of any kind. It is the humility in one that attracts everyone towards himself and in the long run the same humility in one will enable that person to conquer all. The one who blows his own trumpet will never be taken seriously by the others".

Gratitude

"Gratitude is the quality or feeling of gratefulness or thankfulness for the benefit of any kind that one has received. It is the key to true greatness. *Epicurus* remarked "Remember that what you now have was one among the things you only hoped for". Whenever we feel grateful for any blessing, thought, feeling, emotion, word or deed by any one or for anything, in any situation we should never fail to express it. When we fail to express it, is like wrapping a beautiful present and not giving it to the person concerned. It is said to be the master key that opens up all doors of possibility. It is invariably the sign of noble souls and it is the fairest flower that blooms in the soul. Gratefulness is the highest form of thankfulness. Thankfulness may consist in thoughts and words but gratitude shows itself in thoughts, words and deeds. Expressing gratitude also boosts the giver of the boon by making him feel fulfilled. It also develops the quality of humility in the one who expresses gratitude and promotes positive experience in the life of that person".

Self-esteem and Confidence

"Self-esteem is regard for oneself. It has nothing to do with the normal ups and downs of life that are only the temporary fluctuations in the journey of one's life. Self-esteem should not be based upon others' opinion about ourselves. We must have a very clear understanding of ourselves, our nature, emotions, thoughts and feelings. Whether the others appreciate our positive qualities or not should never be an issue. We have to move on in the right path in strengthening our positivity. For one with a low level of self- esteem, the ups and downs of life will have a great impact. Any negative happenings or situations upsets such a person totally resulting in diffidence and a sense of helplessness and a feeling that one is good for nothing, all leading to negativity. It also lowers the capacity to face challenges and the stresses of life in a courageous and in a proper manner and this leads to mental problems such as eating disorders, depression, diffidence etc. Such depressive tendencies can lower and push down the self-esteem levels of any person even further and cause damage in the performance level of the person both at the official as well as in personal relationships. We must never allow ourselves to go in to such moods and feelings. We must have the conviction that we are worthy and can do and achieve any good thing that we desire in our life. This firm faith in oneself leads to positive attitude towards life.

A high level of self-esteem gives rise to and strengthens the confident level of oneself in facing and solving all problems of life. It gives the necessary positive emotional health coupled with happiness. It gives one the confidence that 'one can and one will'. But a very high level of self-esteem may make a person over confident and proud and a low level of self-esteem can make a person diffident and one with low self- esteem. Both are bad. The self-esteem in one should be such that it inspires him to think, say and act in a confident manner without overconfidence or pride or diffidence".

Sincerity and Genuineness

"A sincere person is genuine in his feelings, words and acts. It shows the openness of the heart. It is freedom from duplicity, hypocrisy and all types of pretensions. The person who has these virtues means what he says. He is true to himself. Sincerity encompasses the quality of honesty, genuineness and integrity. Such people will be trusted upon by the others in any type of relationships whether it is personal, social or official. There are people who pose to be sincere without being honestly sincere and genuine. They speak politely, are very courteous and gentle in their speech and actions. But these hypocrites are people whose words come from the throat but not from their hearts. So any act of love or sympathy from their side cannot be genuine".

Optimism

"It is the tendency or attitude to see the positive, the bright, favorable or happy side or the best in everything, everywhere and in every person- to see a glass half full of water instead the glass being half empty and expect the most favorable outcome. It is the tendency to believe, expect that things will turn out and in all probability it will. Winston Churchill said that while a pessimist sees difficulty in every opportunity an optimist sees opportunity in each and every difficulty. To an optimist failures are the stepping stones to success. They do not get disheartened or depressed by the setbacks or failures in their life. Such people have the conviction that every cloud has a silver lining and even the darkest night will end as the Sun is bound to shine the next day morning. They are people who think of the best, work for the best and whatever the outcome they take it as the best for them. They go on with added strength than before and cross over any adversities in their life in the best possible way. This makes them happy and peaceful always. It also brightens life and all get attracted towards such people. But too much of optimism may make a man lazy and he may not put in his best efforts in achieving anything or it may sometime make him expect only the best but nothing less than that. This may lead to disappointments if he does not realize what he expects. So, one should be careful enough to see that he does not become too optimistic in his life".

Equanimity

"It is a state of psychological stability and composure that is never disturbed by pain, pleasure, happiness or sorrow and so on. It is the evenness of mind in happiness as well as in sorrow. People who are endowed with equanimity are calm, composed, and even tempered. They are neither elated nor depressed with anything in life. They view the rich and the poor, the intelligent and the dull, the good and the bad ones equally. It is a balanced state of mind. This nature can be attained only by hard, deliberate, sincere, continuous, and persistent effort in understanding the ultimate reality that all beings are one and the same as everything gets originated and ends up in the same source of Absolute energy from where all have come into this world and we are all the same as that energy though seen differently outwardly at the level of our body and mind. But we are all one at the level of our soul, the energy that is deep inside us. This quality is attained when we detach ourselves from the relative world with all its dualities and when we know that there is only that, that we call the Absolute energy that is divine".

Self-control and fortitude

"It is the ability to control one's emotions, behavior, desires, words and actions especially when negativity overtakes us. These people never enter into any controversy as they remain calm, cool, composed, relaxed under all circumstances because they are endowed with the strength of mind. Fortitude shows the mental and emotional strength that makes a person encounter danger or bear pain or face adverse situations, happenings, and temptations with courage. A person with self-control and fortitude is able to control temptations and distractions of life in a calm manner without getting perturbed. It makes us steady, calm and in full control of ourselves even during highly challenging situations. Self-control requires fortitude or strength of character. Especially one needs a lot of self- control and fortitude to control one's negative emotions. When we think about our goal of life and the consequences of not controlling ourselves then we can understand the importance of self-control and will be in a position to control ourselves under all situations of life. We must also know that to be happy and peaceful in life we have to change ourselves for better. It is said that if you conquer yourself you conquer the whole world. Lao Tzu said "He who controls others may be powerful but he who has mastered himself is mightier still'. Mahatma Gandhi said that "Not to have control over the senses is like sailing in a rudderless ship bound to break to pieces on coming into contact with the very first rock". The senses act as per the dictates of the mind. It is the mind that generates all types of thoughts and then activates the senses for expressing externally all such thoughts".

Patience and Forbearance

"It is a mental state of endurance, restraint and tolerance, under all difficult, adverse circumstances or misfortunes of life or physical pain or mental suffering or any provocation without any complaint, self-pity, loss of temper, irritation, and the ability to control one's emotions especially under very difficult and challenging situations of life. Almost all religions give great importance to patience for attaining spiritual enlightenment. The negative emotions can be tackled to a great extent if one possesses these virtues of patience and forbearance. It is said that "a moment of patience in a moment of anger saves a thousand moments of regret". In short one must be all forbearing like our mother earth".

Charity

"A man's life becomes purposeful, meaningful and worthy only in active charity. Charity made should be such that it should be willingly given from the heart and not for getting any name or fame. Any little act of charity is good because the charity that is a trifle to us can be precious to others. Give what little you can. It is not the quantity of charity that matters but the heart that induces that act of charity. It is like giving light to one who is groping in utter darkness. Charity is giving cheerfully but not grudgingly. As Mother Teresa said, if you can't feed hundred people then feed at least one. Any charity that is extended must be with total love. It is also said, "He who gives early gives twice". That means charity should be made when one is in real need. Again charity should see only the need but not the cause of that need. There is no need to probe the cause as it has no use. See only the present situation and make the charity wholeheartedly.

Some miserly people wrongly believe that by giving away their wealth to others, their happiness will diminish. But actually happiness does not depend upon the quantity of wealth that one possesses. Giving away as much as one can by charity will only enhance his or her happiness. One should forget about the charity that he has made and should have no expectation like recognition, appreciation or praise or gratefulness or indebtedness and so on from the person to whom the charity is made. The charity that tries to proclaim one's goodness in such acts ceases to be charity.

One must pray for the power to give rather than to receive. After all the true meaning of life is to plant trees under whose shade you do not expect to sit. As *Winston Churchill* has said, we make a living by what we get but we make a life by what we give. It is told that once a man came across a beggar and he asked God, "Oh God how can you create such people and do nothing about them"? The God, the creator replied. "I did something. I created you". After all hands are made to contract or hold as well as to open and expand. We should choose to expand our hands to give and to give always. The good that we have done for ourselves perishes with us but the good that we have done for the others remains immortal. As George Washington had said, let your heart feel for the afflictions and distress of those around you and let your hand give in proportion to your purse. It is said that the charitable gives through the door and God puts it back through the window. Charity should not discriminate. Like nature one should go on giving without seeking anything in return. Otherwise charity will seize to become charity as it will only become a business. It should not be made with selfish motive or with pride or for publicity".

Love

"The best exercise for the mind is reaching down to people and lighting people with unlimited love. We know for certain that the most sacred and cherished moments of our life are those that are filled with maximum unselfish love. Even if we cannot do great things it is enough if we do small things with great love. The very look of love and affection will boost the other person to great heights. Everyone can be great provided one has a heart full of grace and love. Just as a heavy downpour of rain drenches the soil fully so also a profuse shower of love overcomes hatred because "Love is a gift to treasure for ever given by God without price tag or measure". When we are able to discover, admit and appreciate the good in others then without our own knowing we bring out the best feelings of love in us. It is said that for loving people it is a loving world and for a hostile ones it is a hostile world. Love also fulfills relationships, increases self-confidence and creates more happiness, peace and harmony for us and for the others. But then love that is possessive is selfish love. It shows the love for oneself. Exhibiting mere sentimentality also is not pure love. Pure love has no place for selfishness. Pure, unconditional love is the ability and willingness to allow those that you love and care to choose to do what they want whether it satisfies you or not, whether they return our love back to us or not. Pure love is letting the other person be what he really is. Albert Einstein said, "A person starts to live when he can live outside himself". Acts of kindness out of love also makes us feel good and valuable. Vivekananda said "All love is expansion". Again he said, "All love is life. All selfishness is death". None lives but he who loves. Feel for the poor, the ignorant, and the downtrodden. It is said, that money does not pay, nor name, fame does not pay nor learning; it is love that pays. To be loved we must be lovable. We must learn to love the heart that hurts us. We never lose by loving. Only by holding back we lose. Mother Teresa once said that there is more hunger for love and appreciation in this world than for bread. When we feel someone else's pain and joy as powerfully as if they are our own then that means that you really love that one.

Love is not a quality that is to be shown to other beings alone. We should also love what we do- our day to day duties, whether it is personal, social or official and so on. We should not do anything just because we have to do it, or because we are compelled to do it. If we do it that way then we can never love the work that we are doing, that is, when we do the work by cursing the work or ourselves for our fate. Whenever we do anything we have to do it in a wholehearted manner with all love. Then its result is bound to be fantastic. Such acts not only create positive energy in one who sends love but also in the other who is the receiver of that love".

Empathy

"Empathy is the ability to understand and experience the thoughts and emotions of the other. It is deep sympathy. It is our ability to experience for ourselves the pain that the other person is experiencing. That means we can undergo the emotional experience of the other. *Ramakrishna Paramahamsa* once said that empathy is a feeling of oneness with the other that the separate identities of yourself and that of the other person lose their boundaries. The other's thirst becomes your thirst, the other's hunger becomes your hunger, and the other's joy becomes your joy. The other is no longer the other but your own self".

Compassion

"Compassion is the highest form of love and empathy. It is translating empathy in to action. It is the ability to support the other through actions during their hard times. It is a feeling of extreme love that cannot be described in words. It is co- suffering. It is a feeling of deep sympathy and sorrow for another who is suffering physically or mentally coupled with the wish to relieve the pain or suffering or misery of that person. Compassion gives rise to an active and intense desire to alleviate the physical or mental suffering of another. It is identification of oneself with the other who is suffering that leads to increased motivation to do something that will relieve the suffering of another. Compassion also induces the feelings of kindness and forgiveness. It is here miracles happen without any effort. According to *Osho*, love purified is compassion. Compassion arises when one enters into the subjectivity of the other person. All religions emphasize compassion. Albert Einstein said "Our task must be to free ourselves from this prison by widening our circles of compassion to embrace all living creatures and the whole of nature in its beauty".

Tolerance

"Tolerance is a fair, permissive attitude towards an opposite view or practices or race or religion or nationality etc. that is different from one's own. It is therefore is freedom from bigotry, the clinging to a particular view blindly. It shows the accommodative or accepting nature of a person. The one who is tolerant finds it easy to recognize, and respect the beliefs and practices of others because he recognizes the dignity of the others as the basis for one's own."

Forgiveness

"The best thing that you can give your enemy is forgiveness. Only one who is broad minded can forgive but not a person who is narrow minded. No doubt it is the way of the world that all help that one extends to another is forgotten soon but the hurt that is inflicted upon that person is never forgotten. But we must determine to be otherwise and there lies our greatness. It is found that there is a healing power in forgiveness. Forgiveness also heals unkind words and acts. We have to forgive everyone for every hurt we have ever received- for our own sake because it creates great amount of positivity in us that leads to happiness and peace. We have to forgive those who injured us so that they as well as we can be happy. Otherwise the negative energy of vengeance will engulf us. Only by forgiving the harm done by others one can live one's best possible life. It helps us to free ourselves from our past and dissolve negative feelings of hatred, vengeance etc. and brings about peace, harmony, hope and joy. This quality also makes us great and magnanimous and helps us in living our life the Best possible way".

Acceptance

"It is the way one receives and accepts the other person's views, and situations as they are without any resistance. It requires a non-judgmental mindset. This virtue makes life very smooth and without conflicts. When one tries to resist then there cannot be any peace and happiness for him. It is also not possible to bring about any change either in other people or in situations. *Lao Tzu* once said "Life is a series of natural and spontaneous changes. Don't resist them. That only creates sorrow. Let reality be reality. Let things flow naturally forward in whatever way they like". As Long Fellow has said, the best thing that one can do when it is raining is to let rain because by resisting we cannot change the situation. The 'let go' attitude is acceptance. The best way is not to resist or fight but allow it to happen. For example when somebody is unreasonable in his argument it is better that we do not contradict. When we resist the irrational view of the other person will only gain more strength. This virtue helps us to bend ourselves a little without breaking during challenging circumstances. In life what cannot be cured must be endured patiently, without any ill will. So also whenever any problem makes us feel miserable for years without any solution then it is better to accept it and say "So what?" or "What if"? And once we become indifferent to such a problem, it will solve itself or it will disappear from our mind on its own accord automatically without any of our effort. We have to stay committed to our decisions but what do we lose if we are slightly flexible in our approach? Only when you swim against the current you get exhausted and drain all your energy. So why can't we swim along with the current and conserve our energy?"

Kindness

"*Mother Teresa* said "Kind words can be short and easy to speak; but their echoes are truly endless". How true it is. But the only thing is that it must be genuine not pretentious. It is said that kindness creates confidence; kindness in thinking creates profoundness; kindness in giving creates love. A kind person has concern for the others. He expresses his kind feeling through his kind behavior. It is the helpfulness to one who is in need for nothing in return. It is good and charitable behavior with real concern for the others. It is true that the language of kindness is such that it can be heard even by the deaf and can be seen even by the blind. It is the emotion of feeling of kindness that bursts through words and actions. We should never miss an opportunity to say a kind word or do a kind act for the others. Acts of kindness make us feel good and valuable. It also gives a sense of contentment, relaxation and happiness and peace. Constant flow of kindness evaporates misunderstanding, mistrust and hostility".

Sympathy

"It is the feeling of concern for the others; perçeiving, understanding and responding to the distress, pain or need of another being. But the expression of sympathy should never be outward or hypocritical. It is the virtue that should emerge from the heart. One can also sympathize with a cause or with a certain point of view of another. In sympathy we feel sorry for the other person or pity them for their misery".

Courtesy, Politeness, Tactfulness and Gentleness

"Courtesy is good manners. It is polite behavior, gesture or remark. Politeness is showing good manners towards others and treating others with warmth and respect. Tactfulness shows itself in polite words and actions. Gentleness makes you speak softly and in a gentle manner without hurting the feelings of others. However, these qualities should not be mere pretentions and therefore hypocritical. They should be genuine. This does not mean that one should bow down to the views of the other. One can disagree with the view-points or attitude of the other but that does not mean that he should behave in a disagreeable manner that is unwanted. He can be polite, courteous, and tactful and still can disagree with the other by talking in a gentle manner. Expressing oneself in a polite and courteous manner in a gentle way will not hurt the tongue in any way. After all you have to treat people the way you want them to treat you and he who is polite, courteous, and gentle is sure to reap friendship".

Thoughtfulness

"It is a feeling of caring for the other having regard for his feelings and needs. It is thoughtful regard or consideration for the others or acts of thoughtfulness by caring the feelings of others. It is treating others the way you want them to treat you. When you offer a glass of water to your co-passenger in the train on midday in summer then it is definitely a thoughtful act; when you extend your hand to lift the one who is below you mentally or physically, even without that person asking for your help then it is your thoughtfulness that makes you act like that. Such acts create a very good feeling in you and a sense of great gratitude towards you in the heart of the other person".

Helpfulness

"The friendly attitude that extends service, help or any assistance to someone who is in need of it is the quality of helpfulness. It is the quality in you that makes you do whatever you can for the others, especially when they are in need of help. It makes life easy for those who are in need of some help as they find someone who can be with them in the hour of need. Even a little act of helpfulness like helping a person to lift himself up when he slips, or the helping the disabled or children or the old to cross over the road that show kindness to them create friendly attitude. Any type of help that is extended- physical, mental, financial, spiritual or moral support to those who struggle go a long way in giving them comfort and help them to get over difficult situations in a better manner as they feel that they are not alone because there is a helping hand to support them. Wise men know the truth that the only way to help ourselves is to help others. Albert Einstein said, " A hundred times every day I remind myself that my inner and outer life depend on the labors of other people, living and dead, and that I must exert myself in order to give the same measure as I have received and am still receiving".

Selflessness

"It is the unselfish concern for the welfare of others accompanied by sacrifice. The one who is selfless, works for the welfare of others forgetting his own needs and comforts of life. This quality absolves man from selfishness, pride, jealousy and so on. A selfless person volunteers his service without any selfish motive of return of any kind. Great achievements by people are born out of great such sacrifices and unselfish service. *Swami Vivekananda* said, "They alone live who live for others, the rest are more dead than alive". Albert Einstein also remarked "Only a life lived for others are worth living". The deepest joy of life and its true fulfillment is experienced only by those who have learned the power of sincere and selfless service. *Buddha* rightly pointed out "we are formed and molded by our thoughts. Those whose minds are shaped by selfless thoughts give joy when they speak or act. Joy follows them like a shadow that never leaves them".

"So, that much about some of the virtues or positive qualities. It is not enough if one knows about positive qualities but it is more important that he imbibes these qualities and puts them in to practice through his constant efforts. Otherwise it will be of no use to anybody. Determine to be positive always by having and following as many virtues as possible. If you determine to be positive always then you will be full of positive energy and that will make you the happiest person in the world. We should not postpone saying any good or positive word or doing any good act as soon as such thoughts click in our mind. Any Postponement may induce you to change our mind for worse. Only negative words and acts are to be postponed as after sometime you will not want them and they will disappear on their own accord".

"Swamiji, how much of positivity one should possess in order to achieve the best possible life"?

"Positivity refers to those virtues that will result in good both in the present as well as in the future for each and every one. The positive virtues are no doubt qualities. But their basis is thought. Only through positive thought the positivity is expressed in words or actions. Thoughts are energy. Unlike matter energy has no volume, shape, size or shape. It cannot be measured as such. Energy can be measured only through the object that makes use of it. For example a 100 watt bulb draws and uses up more electrical energy than a zero watt bulb. But in the case of positivity how much of positivity one is able to create in himself and project it to others cannot be measured but it surely depends upon one's capacity that in turn depends upon his accumulated tendencies of several births, his conditioning and belief systems and more important his desire to improve himself to achieve the best possible life for peace and happiness. However each one of us can endeavor to make ourselves the best possible because man is endowed with the capacity to make himself not only the best possible but the very best by making himself pure and divine".

"Swamiji, kindly tell me about the various methods or techniques that help us in creating and strengthening positivity".

"Positivity can be created and strengthened through various ways both modern and ancient. In modern times there are various methods advocated by the same religion and also by different religious of the world. There are also non-religious methods, secular methods, and scientific methods and so on. In ancient India the traditional methods to bring about positivity included the *Ayurveda* that is the ancient Indian medical science that stressed holistic health for man, *Ashtanga Yoga*, Meditation, *Bhakthi Marga* or the path of a devotee, *Karma Marga* or the path of self-less service and the path of *Gnana Marga* or the path of spiritual knowledge. All these methods try to make man divine and make him experience his life on earth the most beneficial for him and for the others, and also make life worthwhile, purposeful, happy, and peaceful and blissful for one and all."

"It is said that even wild animals become friendly and obey the great souls. We know that the very nature of wild animals is to attack others. Even such animals love great souls. But then how is it possible? It is because these souls overflow with all virtues like sympathy, kindness, love, compassion and so on. When even wild animals can be tamed with virtues why not humans on earth? It may be difficult but not impossible prove the great souls".

"All positive thoughts, feelings, emotions, words and actions bring about maximum happiness and peace of mind to man. Therefore it is essential that we make a beginning towards this at the earliest possible. In worldly life it is not possible for man to fill himself with only positive feelings without any negative thoughts and emotions. But then at least he can make a small beginning at the earliest opportunity. After all, the journey of a thousand miles can begin only with a single step. No one can have all good virtues that are positive but everyone can have at least some virtues if not all. We must only be afraid of standing still but not going slowly. We must make a determination to do something good and positive every day because we get closer to a better tomorrow. We must try to be positive and good and spread positive energy as far as possible for us. Then we will find that happiness running after us. One should also recognize the virtues, the good and the positive in another and learn from the other. But in doing so, one need not and cannot become another. Positivity gives fulfillment as one is able to make his life purposeful and worthy not only for himself but for the others as well and undoubtedly this is the goal of all human beings without any exception because we are not born for ourselves alone. We are here for each other in this world."

5

Mind and its Role

'Swamiji, I understand that the source of both positive and negative thoughts is the mind in us. But what exactly is mind"?

"Even from time immemorial the human mind has been seeking answers for several questions regarding the concept of 'mind'. The ancient seers of India who were spiritually elevated souls pondered over questions like what is mind, how does it function? What are its constituents? how important it is for the overall well-being of man in the world and also for his spiritual enlightenment and they tried to find out answers for these questions through their spiritual quest that included both science and spirituality that walked together hand in hand in ancient India. They revealed their revelations originally in the form of *Upanishads* that also included answers for several other questions about man, the universe and the creative energy that is the cause and the source of all creations.

Today this concept- namely, 'mind' has come to occupy a great deal of attention of the scientists both in medical as well as in the field of psychology as well. This is because of the increasing realization of body-mind-spirit relationships in the overall well-being of man. It has also been accepted that the impact of mind on the physical as well as on spiritual health is tremendous and hence very powerful. A strong, healthy, diseased free body is able to enhance mental well-being no doubt. But even without that, a strong and healthy mind will enable a man to lead a very contented and happy life. This is because mind that is less gross than the body and is also subtle is more powerful than the gross body. The more powerful mind also is able to overpower the pain and sufferings of a body that is weak and unhealthy on account of physical diseases. A healthy mind is a mind that is with as much positivity as possible for one. It brings about mental well-being in one. It also helps one in the *Dharmic* way of living as indicated in the ancient religion of India namely Hinduism. Mental well-being serves as the ladder for spiritual well-being as well. A healthy mind results in physical and mental or psychological well-being and paves the way for spiritual elevation in which one is able to go beyond the mind."

"Mind according to western view is precisely the human consciousness or awareness that originates in the brain and is manifested especially in thought, perception, emotion, will, memory and imagination that are the conscious process that directs and influences mental and physical behavior. It is also the seat of intelligence, the ability to understand and the faculty of thinking and applying knowledge, In short it is the thought process in a being –it enables one to be aware of things, to think and feel and reason out and so it consists of thoughts, emotions, beliefs, and images. The brain is the hardware that allows us to experience these mental states. Mind is also described as a bundle of thoughts and desires, likes and dislikes. According to the ancient Indian view or Hinduism, the oldest living religion in this world, '*Manas*' that is roughly equated with mind refers to the above and also something more".

"What is its nature?"

"The mind is less gross, more subtle, and not visible or tangible like the physical body. Its magnitude cannot be known. Its existence in our body also cannot be seen. It is subtle form of matter. According to *Chandyoga Upanishad* it is formed out of the subtle portion of food. Just as physically each person is different so also they are mentally different from each other. A strong mind can influence a weak mind. Greater the purity of mind greater will be its attraction. Mind is a collection of tendencies or *Samskaras* or bundle of deep rooted habits, desires, conditioning and belief systems, a collection of feelings and perceptions and thoughts. The mind is a fantastic, subtle instrument inside the body of man. It is like a double edged weapon. It can make a person a God or a devil. It can create happiness or misery. It can become a master or a servant. It can create good or bad. It is also turbulent with lots and lots of thoughts that come and go. It is said that human mind is like a new hard drive with no virus that is without any negativity at birth. Later as we grow it is what we feed into that hard drive that corrupts our mind with the viruses of negativity. As Buddha stated we are shaped by our own thoughts. We become what we think. All different emotions are different states of mind. Mind is both divine as well as the devil. It can make one blissful or miserable. It is up to us to choose our life the way we want it to be. Because what we think in our mind we become. We must understand our own mind in order to understand ourselves and the others".

"One's own mind but not that of any other that is one's best friend or enemy. It has the ability and power to push one down into a deep pit or elevate him up to the sky. Mind can also behave like an animal or like a demon, like a human or like divine. When it behaves like an animal or a demon then it degrades one, the possessor of that mind, to that level. It makes a human being either fall down to the level of a beast or demon or helps him to elevate himself as superhuman or divine. Mind is also compared to a monkey as it goes on jumping from one thought to the other".

"Mind is the lord of the senses. It is the mind that activates all the sense organs and directs them to perform their respective functions. The mind directs the senses to perceive, the senses collect and receive the information from the outside world and pass it on the information to the mind back for their further processing inside."

"Mind is also described as the receptacle of thoughts and emotions. Thoughts arise from mind because of desire and desires arise because of the objects and beings outside and also due to the working of the sense organs when the ego gets involved giving rise to attachments".

"In order to get an impartial view of oneself one should be able to make his mind to watch it as an outsider, as a mere witness. Many a time although we become aware of our negative emotions, we try to cover or protect them by justifying our thoughts, feelings, words and actions. This is because we are not unbiased while checking our mind".

"Swamiji, what is the difference between consciousness and conscience?"

"In ordinary usage the term 'being conscious' refers to the state of being conscious, that is awareness or responding to something that is the outcome of the activity of the mind and brain. The state of being conscious is our awareness or understanding of what is happening outside us and within us. When we say that one is not conscious, that is, one is unconscious then it means that his mind through his senses is not registering and knowing all that lies outside himself and his mind also is not active enough to know what is happening within himself. This is experienced in sleep or when one is in coma or in the case of one whose mind and brain are not functioning properly or when one is absent minded, that is, when one is not making use of his mind and brain. On the other hand one is said to be conscious when one is fully aware of what he is thinking, speaking and doing and when one's thoughts, words and deeds are intentional and deliberate. When one is conscious he is fully awake mentally as well as physically".

"In Indian spirituality this term 'Being conscious' is used in a wider sense. In addition to the awareness of what is happening outside and inside oneself, this term also refers to the mental awareness of that supreme ultimate knowledge about what one really is; the knowledge that he is neither the body or mind but the everlasting imperishable self or *Atman*, the innermost energy or the *Atman*, the soul, that is deep inside him, that does not take sides or gets involved in anything but remains as a mere spectator or witness to all that are happening physically as well as mentally outside himself or inside one's being. In addition the term 'consciousness' in Indian thinking also refers to the inner most *Atman* or the soul or the spirit, the very being itself, the everlasting, imperishable one that is in oneself and that remains as a mere spectator or witness".

"The term Conscience refers to the inner sense of what is right and what is wrong. It is the inner voice that guides one towards right conduct and action. It is the inner sense of adherence to righteousness. This term is also used to denote the very *Atman* or the soul that is pure and that resides deep within oneself. People who are virtuous listen to their inner voice that is equated with conscience, our soul or *Atman* and think, speak and act accordingly but those who are full of negativity without listening to their conscience get ruined".

"Will you please enlighten me briefly about the ancient Indian view regarding mind, Swamiji"?

"The ancient Indian sages through their power of introspection could penetrate deep in to the subject of mind and could know what is mind, the existence of mind inside beings, its nature , its ways and subtle workings and so on. They also revealed the various methods to subdue and then master the mind. They also stated that when the mind evolves one can consciously connect his mind to that of others- living or dead and also with the cosmic universal mind. They also pointed out that the root cause of mind is the ego principle. From this seed *Bhuddhi* or intellect came up and from *Bhuddhi* the *Sankalapas* or the will or determination arises".

"The ancient sages of India analyzed the various aspects and states of mind as per the level of awareness, as per their role and as per their functions. The mind is called differently as per its level of awareness, role and functions."

"What are the different states of mind as per the level of awareness"? Will you kindly explain this to me Swamiji."?

"There are five different states of mind as per its level of awareness. These are, the unconscious mind, the subconscious mind, the conscious mind, the super conscious mind and the supra conscious mind."

The Unconscious Mind

"The unconscious mind relates to processes in mind that occur automatically without any conscious effort. In this state the brain functions at its lowest frequency. This has an impact on the behavior of an individual. At this stage the conscious mind is not active because all thoughts, words and actions arise spontaneously or automatically. In the unconscious state of the mind the consciousness is either cannot be made use of or is not made use of. In the case of one who is in a state of coma the conscious mind cannot be used and therefore it is not used. There are also instances when we do certain things in an unconscious manner that is automatically when we do not make use of the conscious mind. Certain acts we do unconsciously due to sheer habit automatically. But there are also times when we forget what we said or done because we fail to make use of the conscious mind at such times".

The Sub-conscious Mind

"The subconscious mind is known as *Chitta* in *Vedantha.* The subconscious mind is in the cerebellum that is located in the hind brain. It takes care of all involuntary activities like walking, writing, eating etc. It is found that the subconscious mind is 30,000 times more powerful than the conscious mind. If only we can make use of its powers properly, then the result will be tremendous. This subconscious mind is the seat of all deep rooted, or suppressed or submerged thoughts that is information and experiences-negative as well as positive. But the negative energy is more powerful though not beneficial than positive energy. That is the reason why we forget any good easily but not the wrong done by another.

The sub conscious mind runs all aspects of our life automatically. It is responsible for the automatically triggered feelings and emotions that one suddenly experiences in one's mind. However it only thinks and converts thoughts into actions from the impressions in the brain cells but cannot differentiate or discriminate good from bad, into positive and negative and so on. The subconscious mind is like a storage room of everything that is not there in the conscious mind. It stores all previous life experiences, beliefs, memories, skills, and all situations of life that one has gone through and all the images that one has seen in his life and so on.

It is said that a new born baby remembers all his past life experiences that are lying in his subconscious mind. As and when he grows up he tends to forget all about his past life experiences. We have been hearing several of such cases. Even western science is coming to admit the fact that there can be something that survives one after the death of his physical body that is somehow connected to a new child. The belief in rebirth is growing even in western countries today and researches are being conducted in this field through past life regression technique that uses hypnosis to recover the past life memories that are buried deep inside the subconscious mind. So by finding out the root cause buried in the subconscious mind one can tackle one's emotions, feelings or thoughts. It is because of the functioning of the subconscious mind that we are able to find solution for some problems all on a sudden- the solutions that has evaded us for so long in spite of trying for it for a long time. After some time the solution suddenly flashes in our mind. This happens especially when the mind becomes calm and quiet. In *Vedantha*, *Chitta* or the sub-conscious mind is compared to a calm lake and the thoughts as the waves on the surface of the lake. In western thinking some equate the unconscious mind with the subconscious mind. The subconscious mind is also called as the subjective mind by some."

"Any thought that gets repeated over and over again will take an imprint within the subconscious mind. Good or bad thoughts that get buried deep into the subconscious mind become the tendencies or *Samskaras* that determine the nature of the succeeding birth of a person".

"The *Vritti* or thought waves arise in the mind and after operating for some time they sink below the conscious level of the mind and settle in the sub conscious mind or *Chitta* as impressions and these create tendencies or *Samskaras* that get deep rooted. The *Vritti* or thought causes *Samskaras* and in turn the *Samskaras* or tendencies also become the cause of *Vritti* or thought waves. The *Samskaras* are in *Chitta* or the subconscious mind. These cause *Sankalpa* that is the will, the resolve, the determination and the *Sankalpas* or the will or the determination in turn causes *Samskaras*. These go on endlessly because in each of one's birth one adds to his *Samskaras* that waits for appropriate experience – bad or good depending upon whether that one had done bad or good in his previous births. All the *Samskaras* or our deep rooted tendencies that form our *Karmas* or actions lie buried deep inside our subconscious mind or *Chitta* in a potential form in a latent manner waiting for an opportunity to come out. After the death of the gross body, the mind in a new body acts in accordance with one's accumulated tendencies or *Samskaras*. Man in order to justify his birth as a human being should try to destroy the evil tendencies and create good *Samskaras* or tendencies through some path or the other that is suited to his nature.

In spirituality it is said that for a self-realized soul all *Samskaras* or accumulated tendencies get burnt away through self knowledge and that such a person goes beyond the cycle of births and deaths because all his *Samskaras* or accumulated tendencies disappear once he gets the self-realization and there will be no more past tendencies for him that gives rise to a new birth and when there is no birth there is no death either. *Samskaras* and birth are like the seed and a tree. Only when there is a tree there is seed and only when there is seed there can be a tree".

The Conscious Mind

"The conscious mind is the source of reason. When our mind is fully conscious we do things with awareness, with full understanding. It is an alert mind. It is that state of mind in which we are aware of all mental processes. The thoughts that arise in the conscious mind are deliberately taken and one is fully conscious about such thoughts. It is the guardian of the subconscious mind and its presence differentiates man from other species of life on earth. It is able to differentiate good from bad, positive from negative with the help of intellect. The best possible life with maximum possible positivity and least possible negativity can be achieved by one by utilizing the power of the conscious mind to its fullest extent as the conscious mind is responsible for all the thoughts that are deliberate, intentional, conscious, and logical".

Super Conscious Mind or Higher Consciousness

"At the higher mind level we are not merely a body-mind but we are soul personalities who go beyond all dualities of life and are totally pure. When one attains this state there is improved attention, and one will be able to live even without food and water for a long time. It is said that the ancient sages of India had performed *Tapas* for many years continuously by inhaling air alone. The enhanced level of consciousness enabled the Sages to transcend all external perceptions and thoughts as the only thought that remained at such a state was about their inner self. At this state the mind shuts its doors to the external world and opens its doors to the inner realm. This is a state when one merges with the inner self without any thought about the outside world or the inner world of dream because the mind at that moment becomes inactive due to heightened knowledge. At this state creativity is the highest. Solutions are found automatically for any problem".

Supra Consciousness State or the Highest Level of Awareness

"The Supra conscious state is the highest level when one goes beyond mind and is not aware of himself including his knowledge about his inner soul. This is the state of enlightenment. At this stage one goes beyond consciousness in the sense of awareness and he becomes an embodiment of total purity- he becomes total purity itself. What remains then is only an experience that cannot be explained in words. Such experience is denoted by the term 'Bliss'. Some people equate the unconscious mind or the state of sleep with supra conscious mind because in both these states one is not conscious of his body and mind. But one should know that in the unconscious state of mind in sleep it is one's ignorance that makes him forget about his body and mind but in the super conscious state it is total awareness or knowledge that makes one go beyond his body and mind as he becomes his real self that is one's innermost spirit or energy".

"Swamiji, will you kindly tell me about the different states of mind as per its qualities"?

"The mind is also differentiated as per its three qualities into *Satvik*, *Rajasic* and *Tamasic*. *Satva* is knowledge, goodness and nobility that are positive qualities. It is purity. The *Satvik* nature likes silence, simple living, high thinking, humility, and lofty ideals in short all that we refer as positivity. The one who has *Satvik* quality purifies his mind and is therefore in touch with the divine.

Rajas is inspiration or the force of action. It also denotes passion. The one who has *Rajasic* nature of mind is passionate, egoistic, quick to react, and engages in verbal dual etc. He also displays both negativity as well as positivity. *Tamas* denotes laziness or inertia. Those whose nature is *Tamasic* are highly ignorant and possess many negative qualities due to their ignorance or lack of knowledge. Man is a combination of all these three mental qualities although their proportions differ in different people. However the ultimate goal of humans should be to imbibe *Satvik* qualities or in a broad sense be positive in our nature to the best of our ability as this alone will justify our birth as human beings."

"*What are the states of mind as per its role?*"

"We can see three different states of mind as per the functions or roles that the mind performs. These are the *Jagrat* or waking, *Swapna* or dreaming and *Sushupthi* or deep sleep states. In the waking state the mind perceives all external gross objects. The mind is extremely active perceiving all external objects and situations and forming thoughts inside with the aid of the physical senses of perception. In this stage both the body and mind are equally awake and active. In the dreaming state the mind perceives subtle objects by creating mental world, objects and beings. All senses get absorbed in the mind. At this state all happenings during one's waking state and the suppressed emotions and thoughts of his subconscious mind come up on the surface of the mind and help the mind in creating dreams of the mental world. In the dreaming state although the mind is awake the body is inactive and sleeps. In the dreamless deep sleep state, both the mind and the body are totally inactive. The one who is in deep sleep is not aware of anything including himself. There is no duality-no good or bad. At this stage, although due to his lack of any type of knowledge, including that of his body and mind he becomes soul conscious without any awareness. He no more identifies himself either with his body or mind. It is like one who is in a coma stage or one who is given chloroform when one does not identify oneself with his body and mind. This is caused due to absence of consciousness that is lack of awareness of his mind of the existence of body and mind that belong to him. At this state the mind is inactive or made inactive. There are neither the worldly impressions nor the creation of mental world at such times."

"Beyond these three states there are two more levels that are not categorized as states of consciousness. These are termed as *Turiya* and *Turiyateeta.* In *Turiya* one gets the glimpse of one's real self-due to his awareness as a result of self-introspection. Beyond this when one is in *Turiyateeta* the mind stops working and one experiences only total bliss where only the pure energy or the soul remains. In this state one goes beyond mind. In this state, not only the mind is totally inactive but the mind also becomes dead and he goes beyond mind and therefore all dualities of life. He goes beyond his consciousness in the sense of awareness and therefore he does not become aware of himself or anything else but only experiences the unlimited bliss that is his own Soul or Atman within himself. In short he becomes his own very self, that is the Soul, the pure consciousness. This experience is beyond all vocabulary."

"Swamiji, kindly tell me about the four functional aspects of mind as per ancient Indian view".

"The ancient Indian sages through their intense and constant meditation found that our mind which they called as *Manas* or *Antha Karana* that is the internal instrument has four functional aspects. These are the lower *Manas* or the emotional mind, *Buddhi*, the intellect that has the capacity of understanding or grasping and discrimination, the *Chitta* or the subconscious mind that is the seat of memory and the source of tendencies or memories and *Ahamkara* or the ego principle that gives rise to self-identification or the feeling of 'I' in man. In *Manas* all emotional thoughts originate. Intellect with its power of discrimination understands and becomes aware of anything and also discriminates anything into good and bad; *Chitta* is the memory of the impressions of past experiences. In *Samkhya* philosophy *Chitta* is included in *Buddhi* or intelligence that is termed as the *Mahat-Tattva*. But according to *Patanjali, Chitta* is mind stuff. *Ahamkara* is the sense of feeling of 'I'. *Ahamkara* or the sense of I' or the ego feeling is where the personality arises because of intelligence and this ego factor is the root or basis of all thoughts and problems in life. This ego is responsible for creating the thought of desire for the objects and beings that are outside one, due to attachment for the objects or beings. This leads to perception, and categorization, and the thoughts, the words and deeds to attain the objects of our desire follow like chain of events. When the ego is destroyed through self-awareness then all problems and difficulties disappear automatically. All these four factors combine to form what is called *Manas* that is in a broad sense translated as mind in English. According to *Bhagavan Ramana Maharshi*, mind is like a man dressed differently in these four garbs. The basis of all these is *Chit* or the *Chaitanya* or the Absolute energy or the effulgence that is the Atman or the soul that is pure consciousness or the inner conscience or energy that is like a witness seeing everything around it. So the source or basis of mind is the individual soul or the *Jeevatman* that is the inner ruler. The mind is activated by this energy and in turn the mind activates the body and makes it perform its functions through organs of senses and perception".

"*Swamiji, will you please tell me about the interrelationship between body and mind*"?

"I repeatedly stressed the fact that the mind and the physical body are closely connected. Mind acts upon the body and the body follows the moods and thoughts of the mind. It is the mind that feels any physical pain or pleasure. A positive mind results in a healthy body and a negative mind results in an unhealthy body. So also any physical discomfort can cause mental ill health and the physical well-being can result in mental happiness thereby mental wellbeing. However it is the mind that is more powerful than the body and as such its impact on physical health is more powerful than the effect of body on mind".

"*What is the impact of food on the mind Swamiji?*"

"The *Chandyoga Upanishad* states that the food that we take is transformed in to three ways. The gross or the heaviest part of it becomes the waste to be excreted; that of the medium density is transformed into flesh and the finest part becomes the muscles. Just as in churning of curd, the finest particles of food rise up and get transformed in to butter, so also when food is consumed the subtlest part rises up and is transformed into mind. Food influences the mind directly. Lord *Krishna* in His *Bhagavad Gita* describes about the three types of food and their effects on the body and mind of man. He says the *Satvik* diet or food that has no intense taste and is pure in all respects calms the mind, gives health and strength to body and mind, and brings joy and cheerfulness to man. It also contributes to serenity of mind, good heartedness, purity of nature and self-control etc. The *Rajasic* food that are excessively bitter, sour, saline, hot, dry, pungent and burning with strong taste excites the mind and it gives rise to pain, grief, disease, passion and so on. The *Tamasic* food that is the food that is stale, tasteless, putrid, rotten, impure dulls the mind. So it is the *Satvik* diet that is most conducive for the physical and mental health of man".

"Food that are taken for merely satisfying the taste of the tongue, taken in excess, taken at short intervals and that are cooked in an unclean manner, that are impure, stale etc. and that are cooked with an agitated mind with tension, fear, anxiety, sorrow, hate etc. surely affect both the physical as well as the mental well-being of a person adversely. On the other hand *Satvik* food that are taken in right quantity that is necessary for a healthy body, taken at proper intervals, at fixed timings, cooked in a happy and peaceful state of mind with the ingredients that are obtained in a righteous manner builds up a healthy body and state of mind. That is the reason why our ancient Indian scriptures give a lot of importance to the food that we take".

"For a worldly person, especially in modern days it becomes highly difficult to follow the pattern of *Satvic* diet all the time. The diet also depends upon the type of work you undertake whether it is physical or mental, the climatic conditions, the place where you live, the tradition you follow and so on. That is why all the religions of the world advice man to go on pilgrimage and visit sacred places like temples, perform various physical procedures of worship to concentrate the body and mind on the divine, reading sacred scriptures and following of what are told in them, having good company only, intense prayers for the welfare of one and all, missing a meal once a day, performing fasting once a week or twice a month, observing various physical and mental disciplines for a particular period before visiting any sacred places like temples etc. observing certain vows relating to our body and mind without unnecessarily torturing the body, self-introspection so that the body and mind will examine especially our bad temperaments so that we can strengthen our positive nature and rectify our mistakes that are in the form of negativities, selfless service for the welfare of all the others , and understanding what are told in the spiritual path through meditation etc. However the effect of food on the body and mind of man cannot be underestimated. Even Lord Krishna in His *Bhagavad Githa* stresses the importance of proper food for elevating one's mind. As I said already, the food that we take not only builds up our physical body but more importantly it influences the mind immensely and makes the mind either pure or impure. Actually food is meant for the very survival of beings in the world. Food plays an extremely important role if our physical body that is gross and in the mind that is the subtle body".

"Although our spirit, the inner consciousness, the divine, that makes the very life that is throbbing inside us, in fact the very life itself is absolutely pure it is being tainted by the impurities of our body and mind. We must wash off the impurities from our body and mind, and should build up a strong body and mind through all means including the food that we take so that the divine, the consciousness inside ourselves can shine in its own glory. Our life will then surely become happy, peaceful, purposeful and worthy and we will be able to do justice for our very birth in this world. If the soul is able to shine in its own glory totally but not partially, then it is like the Sun shining with its original effulgence once the clouds are totally gone and at that very moment man will become God, the divine itself. "

"It is said that mind is a powerful instrument inside man. Swamiji, kindly tell me about it".

"Mind is a very powerful inner instrument. It is like a double edged sword. It is the centre of all good and evil, right and wrong, positivity and negativity. It is said that mind has got the capacity to create or destroy the entire universe in the twinkling of an eye. So the power of mind is enormous and unimaginable. It is said that what you think you become. Mind is the most familiar but yet it is the strangest and the mysterious power that is inside man. We experience our life only because of mind. All sensory organs and organs of actions of our physical body are only tools of our mind. They only obey the dictates of the mind. It is mind that makes the eyes see, makes the ears hear and so on. It activates all sense organs and organs of action. In the waking state when the mind is very active it activates the sensory organs through thought and the sensory organs see or perceive things outside because of the desire or the thought of wanting to see, hear and so on and send back the information to the mind inside. When the mind experiences the information it becomes cognition. The intelligence aspect of mind categorizes the information into good and bad and this distinction gives rise to good or bad feelings or emotions that later comes out as good or positive, or negative or bad words and deeds. Some information gets settled in the mind deeply in memory and comes out as dreams in the dreaming state or come out unconsciously at the most unexpected moments."

"Mind seems to attend many thoughts at the same time. But actually it is not so. It can attend to one thought only at a single moment. It appears to entertain many thoughts simultaneously because the mind moves with unimaginably high speed. It has tremendous velocity. Mind has vast potential no doubt but how much of its power we tap is a great question for which there is no satisfactory answer yet."

"It is the mind that creates good and bad but it is also the mind that helps one to know the ultimate reality. Mind should be used like the match stick that lights the lamp. Once the lamp is lighted the matchstick is of no use. So also is the case with mind. When once the awareness about oneself comes then mind is of no use; on the other hand it is a hindrance because as long as thoughts are there one can't merge with the divine with total awareness. However at such a stage the mind will disappear automatically."

"It is said that the mind has six important powers. These are, *Vedana Sakthi* or the power of perception, *Smrithi Sakthi* or the power of memory, *Bhavana Sakthi* that is the power of imagination, *Miasha Sakthi* that is the power of judgment, by comparing, contrasting etc. the *Sankalpa Sakthi* that is the will and the *Dharana Sakthi* that is the power to know and hold an opinion".

"One can fill his mind with all positivity by making use of the powers of the subconscious and the conscious mind and also by taking advantage of their combined power. Any negative emotion can be removed to a great extent by finding out its cause in the subconscious mind because all emotions are controlled by the subconscious mind. After finding the cause one can deliberately and consciously eliminate such negativity with the help of the conscious mind."

"Whatever you focus, you attract. This is the truth. When you have negative thoughts in your mind you attract negative feelings and negative energy and vice versa. This must be understood by every one of us. The mind follows any habit. So if we make it a habit to think positively about people and situations then we will become positive automatically in a natural effortless manner. Just as water takes the shape of the vessel in which it is poured, similarly, mind also is bound to think as per our habit, as per our desire. It is the mind that creates heaven or hell, happiness or misery for us."

"The power of mind is understood by the Placebo effect that is used by doctors on patients. The Placebo is only a sugar pill used by doctors on patients. But the patients who do not know this think that it is a pill to control or remove their disease. It is found that the rate of success is high in the case of patients who took the pill than those patients who did not take this pill. It only reveals the power of our mind. Those patients who took the pill thought that that pill was given to cure their disease although it was not at all a drug. It shows whatever we believe comes true. This is perhaps the strength of worship and prayer. Psycho kinesis is another technique that proves how powerful the mind is. In this technique the objects are made to move without using physical force but by sheer power of the mind. All these show that one can not only heal his physical ailments with his mental power but one can also make one's life the best possible. In ancient India the sages were supposed to have known the technique of *Parakaya Praveshana* or entering into another body with the power of the mind, knowing not only the past but also the future of themselves and that of others, knowing the past, present and predicting things that will happen in future, Clairvoyance that is knowing about that, that are distant, and so on and so forth by using the power of their mind. They could also subjugate their mind and become its master so that they could manipulate their thoughts the way they wanted".

"As I said, a healthy mind with as much positivity as possible results in good physical health. A good deal of physical problems can also be got rid off by enhancing our mental power. Doctors now believe that most of the physical illness starts from a weak mind. When a person is full of positivity he views life as a blessing because at such a state he is immensely happy and calm and he radiates and spreads positivity to others around him. On the other hand when his mind is filled with negativity he becomes the most unhappy and miserable person in the world and he spreads and radiates negative energy to all the others around him. Pain is experienced only when the physical body is connected to mind. But once the mind dissociates itself from the physical body, for example, when one is in coma or under the influence of chloroform, no pain or pleasure can be felt by the body. So pain is in the mind. It is the thought of pain in the mind that gets reflected in the body as pain. Each thought stimulates a feeling and these emotions whether it is joy or sorrow, pleasure or pain, happiness or misery have their corresponding equivalent in the brain that has a direct relationship with our body cells. The state of our mind can affect our physical body to an enormous extent. A positive mind can work wonders in bringing about the best possible life. This is the reason why all religions and spirituality stress on following the virtues that lead to positive vibrations that ultimately result in a good mental, physical and spiritual health. The modern medical science and psychology also are becoming increasingly more and more aware of the inter connection between mental and the physical wellbeing for a happy diseased free life in the world."

"In modern times man seems to be helpless without pain killers, antibiotics, anti- depression and sleeping pills and so on. The number and varieties of diseases are also on the increase in the modern world. A good deal of physical problems can be got over by enhancing our mental power. The medical science is now coming to recognize the importance of mind or thoughts in treating, and curing diseases of the body and mind in order to restore one's physical and mental health and well-being".

"One cannot only unfold the great powers and the vast resources of the mind but can also utilize and benefit from them by following any path or technique that helps to know the mind, transform the mind and ultimately transcend the mind".

"Is the individual mind connected to other minds in the universe? If so how, Swamiji"?

"As *Swami Vivekananda* had said, each individual mind is a part or fragment of the universal mind. So also each individual soul is a part and parcel of the universal soul. So each mind is connected with every other mind in this universe. Wherever it is located each mind is in communication with the whole world and this is how the thoughts of a person reach another. It is known as Telepathy where the thoughts of one reach another directly. When a person does not resolve to send his thoughts to another, then also the thoughts get dissolved in to the ethereal vibrations that get into the brain and they get resolved again to reach the other person. However it is a roundabout process. That means mind is universal. So a man who understands his mind and has control over his own mind can definitely understand and control the mind of the others without their own knowledge. It is like knowing a lump of clay to know all about a heap of clay. This is how miracles happen. This is how the great sages, the elevated souls could tame even wild animals that are much stronger than them physically".

"We know that with death the physical body perishes. But what happens to the mind after death"?

"Since the beginning man has been desperately asking this question as to what happens to mind after death. In Hinduism that is based on the ancient Indian thinking, it is told that with death the physical body that is made up of the five elements namely, earth, water, fire, wind and space mingles with these five elements in the atmosphere or nature either by burning or burying the dead body and that is the end of it. But the mind with its accumulated thoughts or tendencies survives even after the death of a person. Modern science is also trying to know whether there is life after death. Modern science has made some headway in this regard through the 'near death experiences' and the 'out of body experiences' of the people. They have found out that the near death experiences and the out of body experiences are happening from brain stem that operate in an independent manner. In Hinduism it is told that the mind of a dead person will choose a new body according to its past accumulated tendencies of several births in order to enjoy or suffer as per its past thoughts, words and deeds. All the good or the merits that it had acquired in the earlier births will be rewarded with happiness, peace, success, good physical and mental and also spiritual health and so on and all the bad or the negative or the sin that it had committed are punished with unhappiness, misery, ill health, misfortune and so on while being in the new body. That means all the bad as well as the good that we do will not end with our present life. It is carried forward and this is the cosmic law. If that is so why can't we make efforts to increase all that are positive because not only good will generate good in this life but it will also be carried forward to future births of ours?

When the mind goes beyond good and bad and that is when it becomes totally indifferent to the dualities of life, it becomes totally pure with total positivity and without the slightest traces of any negativity then such a person with an elevated soul becomes one who has not only understood and transformed his mind but also transcended his mind. When one transcends the mind then mind becomes dead for such a person. It is like the body for a dead person. When there is no mind or when the mind is dead then there are no accumulated tendencies because it is the mind that creates tendencies through perceptions. And when there are no accumulated tendencies then there is no more birth and death for such a person. When there is neither birth nor death then there is neither body nor mind for the one who remains as a pure soul and such an individual soul or the *Jeevatma* will merge with the universal soul or the Absolute consciousness that was denoted by the ancient *Rishis* or sages as *Parabhraman* or merely as *Brahman*".

"This knowledge about the power of mind that you gave me now makes me remember a story that I read long ago when I was a child. If I am not wasting your precious time shall I tell you that story Swamiji"?

"Why not? Go ahead. Don't you think that Stories actually make us understand things in a clearer manner and in an interesting way"?

"Thanks *Swamiji*. This story is about a small boy *Ramu*. *Ramu*, a little boy of seven years of age was quite cute and intelligent. But he was also equally timid and lacked self- esteem as he was always feeling diffident in doing anything. His parents were greatly worried about this tendency of *Ramu* because there was no change in his nature and behavior even as he grew older.

Once the grandparents of *Ramu* visited his house and after a few days the grandparents noticed the lack of courage and confidence in him. So one day the grand mother called her grandson to her side and in a whispering tone asked him secretly "Why are you not bold and courageous and confident in your behavior? What is your problem? "*Ramu* with a sad face replied "I do not know grand *ma*. I actually do not know. I know I should not be like what I am now. I want to become bold, courageous and confident about myself. But everything stops at the thought level itself. I am not able to be brave and bold and confident with self-esteem like all my friends. What to do? How can I become bold and strong? I do not know" After uttering these words *Ramu* became very silent. "Is that all? You are unnecessarily worrying about a very small matter. It is nothing. It seems your great grand-father, when he was of your age was also like you, timid and without self-esteem. It seems he was even worse than you. Perhaps you got his nature. It seems one day a sage happened to visit their house and your great grand-father's mother told the sage about her anguish. Immediately he gave the boy, your great grand-father an iron ring after uttering some *Mantra* and then asked him to wear it always and then he left the place. It seems he also asked your great grand-father's mother not to disclose anything about that iron ring to anyone. With all excitement and full faith on that Sage your great grandfather obeyed the words of the sage and he wore that ring at once. Wonder of wonders, it seems, within a few days, there was conspicuous change in your great grand-father's nature and with each passing day he became more and more courageous and bold and his confidence level improved remarkably and in course of time when he grew to become a youngster he became one of the most courageous and bold person with great self-esteem in that entire village. It seems he never parted with that ring until his death. When your great grand-father was in his death bed he called your grand-father to his side and it seems he secretly told all about this ring to your grand-father. Your grand-father showed me the ring after the death of his father and it is then that he told me all about the ring. I have kept that ring safely with me. If you have faith in what I told you and if at all you want to wear that ring like your great grand-father and become courageous and confident then I shall give it to you provided you promise me that you will also keep this as a secret and will never tell anyone about it and also provided you wear the ring lifelong". At once *Ramu* held the hands of his grand-mother and in great enthusiasm he said, "I promise grand *ma*, that I will keep in mind what all you said and will never disclose anything to anybody. Grand *ma*, please give me that ring. I want to wear it now itself". *Ramu*'s grand-mother at once took out that small iron ring from her finger and gave it to *Ramu*".

"A couple of days later *Ramu*'s grand-parents left for their village. After a few days, *Ramu*'s parents and teachers noticed significant changes in *Ramu*'s nature. They did not know what made *Ramu* become very bold and confident all on a sudden. His parents thought that this change in *Ramu* was because of his teachers' encouragement and the teachers in turn thought that it was because of his parents that *Ramu* could become very bold and confident. But when they came to know that neither the teachers nor his parents were responsible for this sudden change for better in *Ramu*'s nature they were puzzled".

"One day as usual *Ramu*'s father was phoning up to his parents and his mother enquired whether there is any change in *Ramu*'s behavior. *Ramu*'s father in great happiness told his mother about the remarkable change that everybody is noticing in his son. When she heard this *Ramu*'s grand-mother began to laugh. Without knowing the reason behind her laughter *Ramu*'s father asked his mother "Why, Why are you laughing?" It is then that *Ramu's* grand-mother told *Ramu's* father, "Did you notice the iron ring that *Ramu* is wearing since a few days"? "Yes of course. What about that ring? What has that ring to do with your laughter or for that matter the change that all of us are noticing in *Ramu* now?" he asked. "It is that ring that did the magic" she said. "Magic? What magic?" asked *Ramu's* father. "O K. I do not want to keep you in suspense any longer. See, when both of us, your father and me visited your house one day *Ramu* came to me and I noticed his face and he was looking sad. When I asked him the reason for it he told me all about his diffidence and lack of courage and how although he wanted to get over them he is unable to change his behavior .It is then that an idea flashed in my mind suddenly. I created a story and after telling him that story I asked him to wear that ring lifelong so that he will soon become courageous and confident. Of course he does not know that it is a fictitious story because I told him that as the real life story of his great grandfather and that worked".

"What is that story tell me now itself" said *Ramu's* father.

"There is nothing extraordinary about that story that I told your son. The small iron ring that I used to wear in my little finger brought all the difference in *Ramu's* nature. I just told him that that ring was given by a *Sanyasi* to his great grand-father who was also timid like *Ramu* when he was young and since he started wearing that ring given by *Swamiji* after uttering some *Mantra* he became very courageous and confident and I asked *Ramu* also to wear that ring always so that he will also become courageous and confident like his great grand-father. I also asked him not to reveal what I told him to any one because once everybody comes to know about it then I said that it will lose all its powers. I know *Ramu* kept it as a secret that's why you did not know anything about that. Any way the purpose is served and that's what all of us wanted. I know you are very happy now as you are no longer worried about your son now, I mean about his timidity. Remember not to disclose this secret to *Ramu*. Let him continue to believe that the iron ring has got the miraculous power as it could change his nature also like that of his great grand-father's."

"This story that I remember even after so many years very clearly make me understand that once the mind thinks and believes something intently with full faith then it will happen as it is bound to happen. Such is the power of the mind. Is it not so *Swamiji*?" I asked.

"Yes, very true" said the *Swamiji*.

After some time I continued with my questions and luckily for me the *Swamiji* also continued answering all my questions very patiently. Now I asked him,

"*What are actually thoughts, Swamiji*"?

"Thoughts are nothing but vibrations of energy and it is a process. These are called as *Vrittis* in Sanskrit. It arises in the mind. Just as waves arise from the surface of the ocean similarly thoughts also arise from the surface of our mind. They give rise to feelings and emotions. As a man thinks so he becomes is an age old proverb. As such they have great power. They shape our character and each moment of our life. It is said that on an average an average person thinks around 60, 000 thoughts per day and 95% of these thoughts are that of the previous day. Like mind thought that arise in the mind is also subtle matter. Like mind thoughts also die when through self-awareness one comes to know one's true identity and when the individual soul or *Jivatma* merges with the *Paramatma* or the universal consciousness or soul or energy. It is a known fact that while negative thoughts give rise to mental and physical illness, positive thoughts promote mental and physical well-being resulting in joy and happiness and peace. No one can lead a positive life with a negative mind or negative thoughts. I repeat a positive mind that contains positive thoughts results in cheerful behavior and a positive, happy, peaceful life while a negative mind with negative emotions and thoughts give rise to a negative, unhappy, and miserable life".

"We build the energy field around us as per the kind of thoughts that we entertain. More and more negative thoughts attract more and more negativity and more and more positive thoughts culminate in more and more positivity and more positive feelings or thoughts because in both the situations the energy field gets stronger and stronger.

As per the law of conservation of energy, energy can never get lost but they change from one level to another. When one's thoughts get projected it affects positively or negatively as the case may. Positive as well as negative thoughts, in the form of vibrations get radiated and reach the other person for whom they are intended and then they return to the sender of such thoughts. So the positive thoughts in one bring about positivity and happiness in the sender as well as in the recipient. So also the negative thoughts bring about unhappiness to the sender as well as the person at whom they are targeted. But if the targeted person has more positive thoughts than negative thoughts in his mind then the negative thought that is radiated from one cannot affect the other person at whom it is projected although he can detect the negative vibrations from the other. Every thought whether it is positive or negative that we release will come back to us in the same form. That means what we send out, we are bound to receive it back. All thoughts that we project inevitably will come back to us with more intensity and speed resulting in strengthening the corresponding energy field. That means we get what we send. According to ancient Indian scriptures that form the basis of Hinduism, the stored up negative as well as positive thoughts in us create the Karmas and they determine and design our subsequent births and this is what they stated as the inherent *Karmas* or accumulated tendencies of the past or the inherent tendencies that form the *Samskaras.* So what we are in this birth is basically the result of our own past thoughts that got converted into words and deeds."

"Thoughts are also are contagious. They are carried through vibrations in space. That means it catches the others and spreads out throughout the world as the thought vibrations travel far and wide in all directions. The thoughts are often compared to a stone that is thrown in a still pond. When the stone is thrown it causes ripples resulting in concentric circles all around. Similar is the effect of thoughts. It is found that electricity travel at the rate of 1, 86, 000 miles per second but thoughts travel in no time. Thoughts can also travel any distance. That is why it is said that the thoughts of prayer can reach one who is living in a distant land or the one who is dead and gone because the distance is immaterial. This reasoning is also the basis of performing *Karmas* for the dead in which it is believed that the positive thought vibrations are bound to reach the dead whether the dead have taken birth in a new body anywhere in the world or whether the souls in the form of their subtle bodies are in the atmosphere searching for a suitable body, suitable birth, suitable family and parents and so on as per their past *Karmas* that formed their *Samskaras* or impressions".

"Why are thoughts given more importance than words and deeds, Swamiji?"

"I already told you that our thoughts go out and radiate from us in the form of energy and any thought whether it is positive or negative that is projected by us after hitting the target return to us sooner or later in the same form. Positive energy will bring back positive energy and negative energy that is sent will come back to us in the form of negative energy. Such energies create similar thoughts in us that make an impression in our subconscious mind and finally become our deep rooted tendencies. Later these tendencies in the form of thoughts are projected and this cycle goes on and on.

Thought is the basis for the creation of good and bad in this world. Actually the entire world is the product of thought only as thoughts give rise to world, beings and objects. It is the starting point of everything in this universe. The scriptures point out that the universe was created as a result of *Sankalpa* or *Ichcha* that is the will or desire or thought of the Absolute principle, the Absolute energy that they termed as *Purusha*. It is our thoughts that create the corresponding words and deeds in one and that make us either positive or negative. The one who has a negative outlook suffers in this world due to unhappiness and misery and the one who has positive thoughts ultimately reaps happiness and peace. So if one wants to be happy and peaceful in this world then he must try to create positive thoughts that lead to positive words and actions. Thoughts, words and deeds look different only at the gross level. In a subtle sense all the three, the thoughts, words and actions are like actions only as the mind creates all the three. However the words that we utter and the deeds that we perform are the result of the type of thoughts that we entertain. Hence thoughts are given more importance than words and actions."

"What are subtle desires, Swamiji"?

"It is the *Vasanas* or the subtle desires that are in the form of waves in the mind that form tendencies. The *Vasanas* or desire is created because of the attraction of objects and beings outside oneself. *Vasanas* exist in seed form. When the *Vasanas* come up on the surface of the mind it causes action for the fulfillment of the desire. The actions in turn strengthen the *Vasanas* or desires. It is the *Vasanas* or desire that causes restlessness in the mind. The *Vasanas* or desire for objects and beings outside oneself create *Vritti* or thoughts for the fulfillment of the desire. The basis of all desires is *Ahamkara* or the feeling of 'I' or the ego. In spirituality desire is compared to fuel and thought is compared to fire. If we withdraw the fuel the fire will extinguish automatically. It is also said that the three pillars of the mind are desire, thought and *Ahamkara* or the ego in us. If we are able to break one link the other two links will be cut off automatically".

"When such is the importance and power of thoughts it is highly necessary that we generate good, *Dharmic* or righteous or positive thoughts in us that benefit ourselves in our life in this world as well as beyond our present existence in this world as they form the accumulated tendencies that decide our future births. They also create similar feelings and generate similar energy, positive or negative in us making our life happy or miserable. Hence there is need to build up positivity and eliminate our negativity with the help of positivity in us. We must think about and practice positive qualities every moment in our life. Then it will become our very nature or character or quality. This continuous practice of positive tendencies or thoughts very soon will become our habit and in course of time it will become our very deep rooted tendencies or *Samskaras* and *Vasanas* or desires that will determine our character for our present life and the nature of our next birth".

"I understand that mind is responsible for both positive or good and negative or bad thoughts. But what activates the mind"?

"While the body, with its sense organs, organs of action and so on is activated by the mind, the mind itself is activated by the inner energy or soul. It is the soul, the inner most energy, that awakens the mind and makes it perform its functions."

"I know that the body, mind and soul make a being but they are different from one another. Kindly explain about their essential difference Swamiji".

"Our body is matter. It has name, form, size, and qualities and so on. It can be seen. It is composed of the five elements of nature namely earth, water, fire, air and space. Once the *Prana* or the inner energy or the soul leaves the body, the body becomes dead and it will have to be disposed off either by cremating the body or burying it and so on. So body has a beginning as well as an end. It has birth as well as death. The body is alive only because of the presence of the soul inside the body. Its organs are activated by soul, the inner energy through the mind. Diseases, injury etc. cause ill health to the physical body. Generally the diseases and injuries are cured by medicines, proper nourishing diet, exercises and so on".

"Mind is subtle matter. It cannot be seen. It has no shape, size, form, name etc. But it has quality; so it generates thoughts that can be either negative or positive. These cause mental ill health or well-being in one. The mental illness can be cured by generating positive tendencies in one by knowing the mind and by transforming the mind. When the body dies mind does not get destroyed but it goes out of the body of a being in the form of accumulated tendencies and it will remain in its subtle form or in subtle body in the atmosphere until it gets in to a new body that fits well with its accumulated tendencies and then it is born again along with the new body. Since it is also matter though a subtle one it can be destroyed by cessation of thought. When there are no more thoughts in the mind then one transcends the mind and mind becomes dead with no more births and deaths. Since both body and mind are matter it needs the support of the soul that is energy for their very existence."

"The soul is the innermost energy in man. It is pure energy with no matter in it. So it has an existence of its own as energy does not need matter for its existence. Even without mind and body the soul exists. But when the body dies the soul gets mingled with the absolute, universal soul and when the mind enters into another body a part of the universal energy again goes inside that being as the individual soul that maintains the new body and the old mind that has entered in to the new body. It is like the air inside a mud pot merging with the air outside once the mud pot is broken and entering into a new mud pot as soon as it is made by the potter.

The soul is all pervading and imperishable. It has neither death nor birth. It does not act. It is highly subtle. Being pure energy, it has no form, shape, size, qualities and so on. It is only an impartial observer or witness of all thoughts of the mind that are expressed through words and deeds and activities. A being is essentially only the soul but not the body or mind and the soul being pure energy it can neither be created nor destroyed like the body and mind. It remains the same forever."

"I have also heard the spiritual masters telling that we are composed of three bodies namely, the physical body or the Sthula-Sareera, the mind or the subtle body that is Sukshma-Sareera and also the causal body that is the Karana-Sareera. I can understand about the body and our mind. But what is the causal body or Karana-Sareera and what is its role?"

"Causal body is the cause of our physical body and mind. This causal body envelops the soul with ignorance. It is a vehicle through which one comes to know about his real self, the soul. The one who is in the spiritual path tries to pierce through the causal body that is nothing but ignorance to know the true effulgence of the soul".

"The gross physical body or the *Sthula-Sareera* that is made up of the seven *Dhatus* or ingredients like muscle, bone, nerves etc. has form. It also undergoes many changes from birth to death like growth, decay or decline and old age. But our *Sukshma-Sareera* that is our mind has no form although it also undergoes changes like our gross body as we feel and think differently at different times. Sometimes we feel happy while at some other moments we feel sad. All the dualities of life are experienced by our mind through our senses of our physical body. The causal body or the *Karana-Sareera* is nothing but ignorance or the veil that covers the true effulgence of the soul. It is because of this ignorance that we associate ourselves that is the soul with our body and mind. Once knowledge comes the veil of ignorance vanishes and man is able to realize that he is not his body or mind but the soul, the consciousness itself".

"During waking state that is *Jagrata Avastha* all these three namely, the gross, subtle and causal bodies are fully awake and are active and this makes us perform our functions through our organs of senses the *Jnanendrias* and organs of actions, the *Karmendrias* by associating ourselves with everything in this world that are external to our body. The causal body that is ignorance makes us believe that we are the body.

However during dream state that is *Swapna Avastha* our physical body becomes passive and inactive while our mind and the Causal body alone remain active. The thoughts that are submerged in our subconscious mind not only of the present birth but also of several past births come up on the surface and they become dreams. Our causal body that is our ignorance during this state of dream makes us believe that what all are happening in our dreams as the actual happenings. Only after waking up we realize that it is not so.

During dreamless sleep that is in *Sushupthi* both our physical body and mind become passive and inactive and only our causal body that is our ignorance remains awake. During such a state of deep sleep that is dreamless sleep we become one with our consciousness, our soul that is our *Jeevatma* and we enjoy the bliss or *Ananda. Ho*wever our causal body that is our ignorance that is awake even at this stage does not allow us to know that bliss. Only after we wake up we come to know that we had a very good peaceful sleep.

Beyond this is the experience of *Turiya* in which one becomes fully conscious and therefore totally aware that he is really the soul and nothing else and in this supreme consciousness with total awareness he enjoys the bliss or *Anada* that is the real nature of our soul or Atman. This is experienced only by those who are spiritually elevated. At this stage one is able to pierce through the causal body that is ignorance and attain real knowledge about the self. The knowledge like light removes all ignorance that was like a veil that was hiding the soul from our understanding of the soul or self or the very consciousness that is what we really are.

Beyond even this *Turiya* experience one becomes the very Bliss itself that is *Atman*, the soul. This is the Supra Conscious state. He becomes one with the bliss and therefore only the experience remains as the experience and the one who experiences the bliss and that which is experienced become one and the same without any distinction. This experience comes only to the purest ones who are well advanced spiritually".

"Even an average worldly person can enjoy and experience the inner happiness and peace through knowledge that is the light that removes the darkness created by ignorance. Knowledge about the dualities of life, how to tackle them etc. coupled with a sincere determination and effort will surely enable a person to transform his mind in such a way that he becomes capable of eliminating the negativity in him and at the same time increase his positive qualities and tendencies even during his waking state. Once he is able to achieve this goal then automatically he will be able to enjoy the inner happiness and peace that he craves for in his life".

"Swamiji, how can the soul, the consciousness that is pure, make the mind think negatively?"

"No doubt mind is responsible for thoughts that are good, positive and virtuous and also for thoughts that are bad or negative or that are categorized as vices. It is also true that the mind in turn is woken up or activated by the soul or our inner consciousness. For both mind and body the source is the inner energy, the life force, the soul, the consciousness. But the soul does not give any instruction to the mind nor does it direct the mind to perform either positively or negatively. This is because the soul, or consciousness or the inner energy is only a pure energy that does not categorize anything as good or bad. It does not make the hands perform good or bad actions or instruct the mind to think good or bad or the internal organs operate properly or otherwise. The soul only activates the body through mind. It is up to the beings to make use of their intelligence and think, speak and act positively, and make the internal or external organs perform in the most desirable way resulting in maximum peace and happiness for oneself and for those around oneself. It is our ignorance that makes us think that we the inner soul is the mind and body. It is the mind that thinks good or bad but not the soul. The soul or consciousness is only an impartial witness that sees the play of body and mind. While the body may enjoy any food that is not conducive to its health, the mind similarly may entertain any negative thought that is not conducive to one's mental health. It is up to our intelligence and discretion to make use of our mind and body in a proper manner so that one's life becomes a blessed and fulfilling one".

"The limitations are only for the body and mind but not for the soul. Body is totally matter and mind is subtle matter and only matter has limitations, name, form, qualities and so on. The inner energy or soul is totally subtle and pure. It is only pure energy and therefore it has no form, name, qualities and so on and hence no limitations. So, one must know that it is not the soul that makes the body and mind perform positively or negatively, although it, the soul, is responsible for their very existence. How can the parent of a grown up son who has a will and desire of his own and is endowed with the intelligence to differentiate between the good from bad and who enjoys the freedom to choose either good or bad be responsible for the actions of the son even though the parent is responsible for the birth of his son?"

"It is also true that it is the Absolute soul that enters into the body of an individual and becomes the individual soul. *Maya* or ignorance covers the purity and power of the individual soul or the *Jeevatma*. Ignorance is caused because of the sense of ego that gives rise to desire, attachment, and expectations etc. that arise in the mind of man. Mud is the basis of the mud pot. If one due to his ignorance wrongly thinks that the pot is the basis of mud then he attributes all the qualities of the pot to the mud. Similarly the Universal soul that is inside the body of man as the individual soul that is pure is the basis of body and mind. If one wrongly thinks due to his ignorance that it is his body and mind that make up the soul then he attributes all qualities of the body and mind to the soul. As *Swami Vivekananda* said, every soul is a Sun covered over with clouds of ignorance. There is no loss of power in the sunshine. But the total power of the sun is not seen because the sun is covered by clouds. When the soul energy that is inside the body of a being is seen in its original power by removing the cloud of ignorance through knowledge that is, the light that removes darkness or ignorance, then it will shine in its own original purity inside man. All thoughts that arise in the mind of such a man of wisdom are bound to be totally pure and therefore positive. The thoughts of an average worldly person are a mixture of both good or positive and bad or negative. So it is ignorance that makes man think that the soul is responsible for any negativity in man as the soul that is actually pure can never prompt anything bad or negative."

"How can our thoughts bring about mental well-being?"

"Thoughts arise in the mind and the mind is only an instrument like the body. We can make use of the body the way we want and to a certain extent it is in our power to make our body healthy or otherwise. Food that is healthy, consumed in required quantity and at proper intervals for maintaining the body and sufficient exercises and rest for the body result in a healthy body. On the other hand food that is harmful to the functioning of the internal organs of the body are consumed or when food is consumed in excess or less than the requirement of the body or when one does not have sufficient sleep or also exercise then ill health will be the result. That means we must know about our body well and act in a proper manner so that we enjoy good physical health. We must be fully aware of all that are good and bad for the body and choose only that, that is good and promote body health. Same is the case with the thoughts in our mind. We must know which types of thoughts are good and which types of thoughts are bad and act accordingly. When Proper nourishing thoughts that are positive are entertained in the mind then one becomes mentally happy and peaceful. On the other hand bad and negative thoughts will make one mentally ill by making him miserable and unhappy. Just as we must know about our body and take care of the body in a proper manner to enjoy good physical health, similarly we must also know what thoughts, words and actions are good for ourselves as well as for the others and entertain only such thoughts because that only give man mental health through peace and happiness in life. A person with sound physical health not only will enjoy his health but also will be able to turn out more work and his dependence on others also gets reduced as and when he becomes more and more healthy physically. Similarly in the case of mental health, the one who nurtures more and more positive thoughts that are nothing but virtues and less and less negative thoughts that are only the vices will enjoy more mental health. Such a person who radiates positive vibrations will attract each and every person towards him. It is natural that human beings crave for love, affection and appreciation from all around them and the one who projects these thoughts is bound to receive all these in return. This will encourage and inspire him to do more and more good to others through his positive thoughts and his mental well-being will increase".

"What is the connection between our thoughts and the saying 'As we sow we reap'?"

"When you sow the seed of a mango tree you can expect only a mango seedling from that but not any other seedling. Similarly when you plant any positive thought in your mind and send out positive vibrations then in due course these vibrations after reaching the target return to you back making your life happy and peaceful. So also when you plant the seed of a poisonous plant you can expect only a poisonous seedling from that. Similarly, when you send negative vibrations by planting and sending negative thoughts then they are bound to return to you sooner or later in your present or future birth making your life unhappy and miserable with no peace. That means what you sow you are bound to reap. This is what the law of *Karma* of the Hinduism says".

"By preventing creation of negative thoughts in the present and by generating and projecting positive thoughts in the present one may be able to make his future happy and peaceful. But what about the already created and projected negative thoughts, words and deeds of the past that have their negative effects now in the present? Can one undo the effects of past negative thoughts that make him suffer now by atoning for all the bad that he had done in the past?"

"So, you want to know whether one can settle his *Karmic* account of his past. The ancient Indian scriptures compare our thoughts, words and deeds to a released arrow. The released arrow cannot be manipulated to change its direction or intensity. So whatever negative thoughts that we had that formed negative words and negative actions in the past are bound to come back to us sooner or later. There is no escape from that. But with awareness one comes to know that he, but nobody else is responsible for all the negativity that he faces now. So he will not blame God or others or situations for his present unhappiness. This awareness, this knowledge helps him to improve himself with positivity that ensures him a happy future. Incidentally it will help him to accept any negativity from others or situations in the present in a graceful manner with a positive outlook without returning negativity for negativity but by returning negativity with positivity.

The Hindu scriptures also are full of examples of people who performed penance in some way or other to atone for their sins-that means to undo their negativity of the past. Penance is self-imposed punishment. If one tries to atone for his sins by penance then it is bound to elevate his soul and make him pure and a pure mind is far above any duality. So the effects of his past negativity that shows itself in the present in the form of sufferings and pain will fail to affect him the least because he goes beyond all life's pleasures or pains. Another important way is to generate and follow positive virtues that will make one purer and purer and no suffering can affect a pure soul because the one who has purity will have equanimity of vision. He will view all pleasures as well as miseries of life in an equal manner. Under such circumstances one can also seek the divine help by making himself eligible for such blessings through his positivity. He may also through prayer and meditation receive the required knowledge. His faith and devotion to the Almighty gives him the conviction that God or the divine energy will protect him and help him in facing all his present hardships on account of his past negativity. This thought gives him immense moral support and he does not feel the pinch of the effects of his past negativity anymore because as one thinks he becomes. He may also through meditation receive the required knowledge about the root cause for all his present problems and accept and endure without the slightest traces of self-pity or misery, the effect of his past actions without blaming anyone for that. He may also make his mind pure through selfless service and make himself happy so that he gives the least importance for the results of his past negativity. In this way one goes beyond the effects of all his past negative thoughts, words and deeds which we usually categorize as the sins committed."

"The scriptures ask man to be the master of his mind but not its servant. Why is it so, Swamiji?"

"*Patanjali* in his *Yoga Sutra* says that it is the Mind or *Chitta* that holds the key to ultimate reality. The mind can serve as a doorway or a barrier, a vehicle of spiritual enlightenment or an instrument of enslavement".

"No doubt our mind has immense power to shape any type of thoughts, either positive or negative. It is up to us to make our mind think positively and avoid thinking negatively. For this we have to make our mind to listen and to obey us, our inner voice, that is our true self. Our true or real self, our soul, the consciousness that is deep inside us is different from our body and mind. Our sense organs and organs of action get activated by mind. When we are asleep mind is also asleep so our sensory organs and organs of actions do not get activated. But as soon as the mind wakes up it starts activating the sensory organs and organs of actions and they are made to start their respective functions and the mind itself also begins to think, and various types of thoughts arise in our mind. Mind therefore is inevitably the master of all the sensory organs and organs of actions. But then who is the master of the mind? Who and what activates the mind? After all mind also is an instrument like our body. While the body performs by speaking, doing both good and bad and so on the mind thinks, remembers, understands, discriminates and has emotions and feelings both positive and negative and so on because after all it is also only a tool. While the body is the tool of mind the mind also must be a tool of a greater power or energy. If so what is that power that can control and dictate the mind? The answer for this question is given by the great ancient sages of India".

"As I told you already, the mind or *Manas* has four functional aspects namely, *Manas* or the lower mind or the emotional mind, *Buddhi* or intelligence, *Chitta* or the sub-conscious mind that is the seat of the accumulated tendencies and *Ahamkara* or ego that is the sense of the feeling of 'I' in man. When a man follows any of these or all these aspects then there is no guarantee that he takes the correct decision or acts in a proper manner. That means one should not ultimately depend upon his mind for taking any decision because mind is very tricky. There is every possibility that these four aspects of the mind may induce man to take biased decision, that is, if he listens to the dictates of emotion, intelligence, accumulated tendencies of the subconscious mind ,the ego sense, his desire and his belief systems of his present birth that we call as conditioning of his mind".

"When we perceive any information from outside then it goes into us and becomes a thought that gets settled in the mind as impressions and this gives rise to some type of emotions. More and more of such thoughts get settled in the mind and these form the tendencies or the inherent nature of a person. When anything is perceived by the senses at the command of the mind then the information goes inside us. Later the intellect discriminates the information received through the sense organs. If the emotional mind dominates then intelligence gets blurred. Under such circumstances, if the emotional mind thinks something as bad or negative then it is confirmed as negative by intelligence and vice versa. If that part of the mind that is intelligence over powers the emotional mind that is another part of the overall mind then as per its analysis the thoughts are categorized as good or bad. When the intellect at one moment discriminates something as good then all positive thoughts flow from the mind but at another time the same thing when the intelligence discerns as bad then we think negatively then negative thoughts flow from the mind. The emotional mind takes quick decisions on the basis of emotions. But the intelligence that has the discriminating ability, if it acts independently then can either confirm the decision of the emotional mind or not. This is possible only when intelligence takes an upper hand. But in creating and projecting positivity that need an emotional attitude it is better to follow the emotional mind coupled with intelligence. For example when a person is to be saved from being drowned in water then spontaneous action is required. At such times one has to take quick decision as per the dictates of his emotion as well as intelligence. If one merely goes on analyzing whether he has to leap in to the water to save the person or not then by the time he decides the person will get drowned in the water. But when any negativity creeps and tries to project itself or when any deliberate decisions are to be taken then it is better that intelligence takes the ultimate decision without allowing the emotional mind to take an upper hand. One who has a low level of intelligence may either yield to emotional mind because of his incapacity or will that makes him not to listen to it without knowing the value of the emotional mind in taking correct decisions whenever spontaneous emotional acts are required. But when one is able to listen to his inner voice then directly he will get the answer that is unbiased and correct. This is because even when any one takes the help of emotional mind that is the lower mind, and that of intelligence that constitute mind then there is every possibility that he may go wrong in his decision because mind is very tricky as it can make either the emotional mind or intelligence or both of these act in a biased manner by justifying one action or the other. Therefore, one should not listen to one's mind because if he does so, then he will not be able to act in an unbiased manner. But one can surely take into account the arguments and justifications that are put forth by both the emotional mind and intelligence. But taking any ultimate decision on the basis of these two will not result in right conduct always. Just as a judge after listening to the arguments put forth by the lawyers takes his own decision finally, similarly, we should also listen to the emotional mind and intelligence but act as per the dictates of our inner voice. When one acts like this then he makes use of his mind as a tool but never allows the mind to take any decision. So any one will be able to take correct decision and act only when he listens to his inner voice but not the mind".

"One should also know about that part of mind that is the Ego or *Ahankara*. It is ego that gives rise to attachments and expectations that leads to many negative tendencies in man. That is the reason why spirituality stresses on egolessness or humility if one wants to be mentally and spiritually happy that results in physical health as well. A person who is egoistic does not achieve anything in his life and becomes a failure because such a person thinks only about himself. He can view everything only subjectively but not from other's point of view and this results in selfishness that give rise to many negative emotions. So, one should not act as per the dictates of his ego sense of his mind as well. If he does then such an act also will not be unbiased and correct".

"*Chitta* or the subconscious mind is another functional aspect of mind. This creates tendencies or *Samskaras* in one and if one acts as per his tendencies of the past several births then such an act need not always be unbiased or correct because any negative tendency in one will induce him to act negatively only".

"Another important aspect of mind is its desire. Like the emotional mind the *Ichcha* or desire also is not totally bad or totally good. If there is no desire then nothing can be achieved in life. Even the basic needs of man cannot be fulfilled if there is no will or desire. But the scriptures say that desire should be kept within limits- especially the desire for material wealth. This is because too much desire that leads to craving will only result in harmful consequences to man. The ancient scriptures also point out that desire as such is neither good nor bad. What matters is what one desires in life. Again the scriptures say desire is natural to man. But it is the expectation of results that causes all anxieties, tensions, and disappointments or over joy in man that is dangerous and that cause negativity like misery, depression, disappointments etc. Even if any material desire is fulfilled it is natural that some other desire will come to the forefront seeking fulfillment. So it is a never ending process. None can fulfill all his needs and wants. The scriptures therefore point out that man can have material desires because it is only natural instinct in man but one should keep his desires within limits and he must also be indifferent about its results. But usually we desire something and work for it physically or mentally with the expectation that we will get the desired result. But if the outcome is different then we get disappointed, depressed, dejected and so on and these create negativity in us that is harmful. If on the other hand if the outcome is as per our expectation then we are induced to desire more and more and that also may lead to adverse consequences because every time our wish may not be fulfilled. So, when we act as per our desire then also it cannot be unbiased and correct."

"Still another important factor is one's conditioning or belief system since the time of his birth. A child who is born in a good family, having parents who are virtuous and studying in a school where ethical and moral code of conduct are stressed and taught, who is in the company of good friends and having neighbors who care for the welfare of others and living in a society that gives importance to righteous living accumulates positive tendencies and his mind will try to look everything positively only as he grows older because positivity will become his very nature. On the other hand the child who is growing in a surrounding and in an atmosphere that is contrary to this is bound to develop all negative tendencies and mind also will act as per his conditioning. That means if he acts as per his nature then also such acts may not be correct and unbiased".

"So, that means correct decisions cannot be taken if one allows his mind to dominate him because the emotional mind, intelligence, the subconscious mind and the ego sense that constitute the mind coupled with one's desires and his present belief system or the conditioning factor may not give an unbiased and correct picture of anything that one thinks. That means one should not yield to the dictates of his mind instead he should make his mind obey him. Only when he listens to his inner most voice he will be able to view anything correctly and in an unbiased manner and only when he acts as per the dictates of his inner voice he can act properly and correctly. That is why it is said that one should become the master of his mind but not its servant and listen to his inner voice without yielding to the dictates of one's mind."

"Is the mind good or bad actually".

"Like body, mind is also an instrument. It is neither good nor bad but it can become good or bad with its proper or improper usage. It is like a knife. When the mind is made use of in a proper manner it yields wonderful results. A knife if it is in the hands of a great surgeon will save the life of a person. But the same knife when it is in the hands of a murderer leads to dire consequences. So actually the problem is not with the knife. So also the problem does not lie with the mind. The problem arises because we do not make use of the mind in the best possible manner that will yield the best results. Blaming the instrument is of no use. So one should, through awareness know how to make use of the mind for achieving the best possible results. One can make use of his physical body for his own wellbeing and for the wellbeing of the others or he can make use of the body for his own destruction or for causing destruction of the other beings. Similarly mind also can either think good or bad causing mental well-being to himself and for the others or for causing destruction for himself and also for the others."

"Since mind has these opposite qualities it is essential that we dictate the mind as to what it should think. Since we know that positive thinking is the only way to bring the best possible life that is full of happiness and peace we should make our mind think only the virtues of life that leads to this goal. On the other hand if the mind goes on its own way like a let loose horse then it will wander everywhere with all kinds of thoughts including the ones that are wasteful, useless and negative that ultimately will deplete the energy in us and there by weaken us. That is why it is said that we have to take control and subjugate our mind and become its master and train and discipline our mind to think positively for reaching the goal of peace and happiness in our life".

"*It is said that one should listen to his inner most voice but not the mind. What does this mean Swamiji?*"

"The inner voice is that power or energy that guides us properly to choose the right path. It is the individual soul, our consciousness, the conscience in us, the inner energy, the real self, God, the *Jivatma* or the individual soul that is *Paramatma* or the universal soul inside a being. It is like the life energy that is inside the seed that later grows into a big tree. The seedling of any big tree comes out from this life energy that is inside a seed after the outer layers of covering of the seed are destroyed once the seed is sown into the soil. But if one tries to peel off the seed in order to find out that energy that is inside the seed that is responsible for the big tree then one cannot hope to get the seedling even if he plants that that remains after peeling off all the outer layers of the seed. This same energy is also responsible for the creation of everything in this universe whether the universe itself or the beings or other things in the world that is not manmade. Even man makes anything only with the help of what is available in nature as he cannot create anything from nothing. This life energy is highly subtle and it cannot be seen. It is the power or energy that activates both mind and body. This innermost energy in the core of a being pervades all through the body and mind like butter in curd or butter milk. When the allotted time of existence of the body in the world is over this individual soul goes out of the body and gets mingled with the all-pervading energy, the *Paramatman* or the Absolute. The individual soul is like the water inside the bubble in the wave of the ocean. When the allotted period of life of the bubble is over then the bubble bursts and the water inside it gets mingled with the vast expansive ocean losing all its separate identity as a bubble. With the death of a person the individual soul goes out of the body and the mind also as the accumulated thoughts or tendencies leaves the body along with it".

"To achieve the best possible life that culminates in peace and happiness for man, one should make his mind listen to the dictates of one's own pure consciousness, that is devoid of any type of ignorance. The individual soul, the *Jivatma*, or the inner voice will never go wrong as it does not take sides because it is only a mere witness to everything that goes on. Many a time we think that mind is our inner voice and we have to listen to our mind. But in reality it is not so. Mind is only a subtle tool. It can either do good or bad. But it is a very good tool that helps us to listen to our innermost voice- our soul. However mind is not a witness. It can take sides. It can either ruin us by entertaining negative thoughts and later by justifying the entire negative in us or enhance our positivity by encouraging and inducing positivity in us. One should not listen to the dictates of one's mind although it is the most powerful organ in one's body. Like a master we should try to make use of, direct and dictate our mind, to go deeper and deeper inside us so that we can touch the very inner core of our being, the consciousness, the innermost subtle, invisible inner voice and listen and obey its commands only. Our mind should be made to listen to that inner voice of ours and become our servant and not our master. So if mind is made use of properly then the mind itself will make us listen to that inner most voice. It is mind that connects the outer world with our inner being. Without mind one will neither know anything about the outer world or about the inner self- the inner being or the inner self that activates both body as well as the mind with all its constituent elements."

"If only we can listen to our innermost voice, the voice of our soul, then it will show us the right path to reach our goal of Peace and Happiness through the best possible life. The one who has a firm faith and conviction in that will be able to listen to its silent voice provided he makes himself eligible to hear it by being pure and positive to the best of his ability. Such a one not only is able to get answers for all his queries but is also able to face and solve all the problems of his life in an easy and effortless manner because the inner energy or the soul takes all the responsibilities on his behalf".

"*How can one know whether he is becoming aware of the commands of the mind or that of the innermost voice? How to distinguish between the mind and the inner voice*"?

"The prompting of the inner voice has no basis. It comes on its own accord. It does not discriminate anything into good and bad like the mind. It is like a witness and therefore is impartial; it does not take sides; it neither condemns you nor praises you. It is understood all on a sudden in a spontaneous manner without any thinking. But mind is partial, biased, takes sides, and tries to justify our actions. The promptings of the mind comes from deep rooted or present emotions and thoughts. Only by making oneself more and more pure and by entertaining all values and virtues, one automatically without any effort is be able to understand and listen to that innermost voice. But mind also thinks good not only bad. And when it thinks good then only good will come out of it. So whenever we are in a dilemma, not knowing what is right and what is wrong then we have to leave the decision to the inner voice but not to the mind because the inner voice will never allow us to grow astray. It will never mislead us. Then what is the difference between mind and the inner voice?

Mind is both human as well as divine whereas the inner voice that is pure is only divine without any blemishes. If we are sincere, honest and humble enough in our efforts to become the best possible human beings and work sincerely for eliminating the negativity with as much virtues or positivity as possible then the inner voice, that is nothing but the soul inside us, our consciousness that is pure and divine will shower the necessary blessings and grace upon us automatically even without our asking and we will be able to achieve the goal of the best possible life very easily. Such a situation can only be experienced but cannot be explained in words as the experience is beyond all vocabulary. As *Osho* has stated, there are times in our lives when too many voices seem to be pulling us this way and that. Our very confusion in such situations is a reminder to seek silence and centering within and listen to the inner most voice that does not speak in words but in the wordless language of the heart. It is like an oracle who speaks only the truth".

6

Paths for Peaceful and Happy Living

"Swamiji, what is meant by holistic health approach"?

"If a man has to be happy and peaceful in life and enjoy his life to the maximum then it is highly necessary that he possesses a good physical, mental and spiritual health. That means there must be harmony and overall well-being of body, mind and spirit. When there is physical health it leads to mental health and when there is mental well-being it leads to physical well-being as well. The spiritual well-being depends upon the physical as well as mental well-being of an individual".

"The holistic health approach is an approach towards the overall wellbeing of a person that addresses the body, mind and spirit or the physical, emotional or mental or psychological and spiritual aspects. It is a complete and an overall approach to all the three namely, body, mind and spirit. A holistic approach does not view the body, mind and spirit as separate entities. This approach promotes drugs, medicines and surgery only when it becomes highly necessary or absolutely essential for the body. Instead it analyses the causes of the disease, its symptoms and its cure not only at the level of the body but also at the level of the mind and the spirit as well. Thus it takes into account the mental and spiritual aspects in improving one's physical health. Similarly for an improved mental and spiritual health or to ward off any mental illness due to negativity found in one or due to blockages of energy in one it goes in to the root of the cause that may be found at the level of the body and also at the mental level namely the psychology or mental makeup of a person and also the spiritual understanding of the person and after analyzing one's nature in this way it tries to remedy any situation of mental sickness. That means all these three namely, body, mind and spirit cannot be viewed separately as they are closely inter related or inter connected since what affects or benefits one will affect or benefit the other two as well. Therefore it is necessary that one enjoys an overall wellbeing in which body, mind and the spirit are healthy as a whole where there is harmonious functioning of body, mind and spirit. That alone will bring the best possible life for man leading to peace and happiness for him".

"What is meant by 'Alternative or Holistic medicines'? What are the various methods and techniques that bring about holistic health?"

"Alternative medicines are any form of medicines that lie outside the main stream of medicines particularly western or Allopathic medicines. It is estimated that there are more than 100 systems of alternative medicines in practice all over the world today. Since it is based on the interaction among the body- mind-energy or spirit it is called as holistic medicine. Some of the modern practices like, Naturopathy, *Reiki*, *Pranic* healing, Aroma therapy, Acupuncture etc. are based upon the ancient Indian wisdom. Naturopathy is an age old Indian wisdom that says that the body when left to itself can heal all its ills because of the play of the inherent natural defense mechanism of the body that are self-curative and self-preventive. It is therefore called as nature cure. Naturopathy involves hydro therapy, exercises, fresh air, sunlight, herbal remedies and so on. *Reiki* is an energy healing system. It is also called as palm healing or hands on healing system. In this method the universal energy is transferred to the person through palms for self-healing and for a state of equilibrium. It is based upon the ancient Indian wisdom that thoughts have the power to direct energy. This system heals by raising the vibrations of energy of the being. It heals physical, mental, emotional and spiritual problems or ailments with the knowledge that when the flow of the life force or energy is disrupted, weakened or blocked then mental and physical problems are bound to result. *Pranic* healing is an ancient Indian technique of healing that utilizes *Prana* or life energy to heal the visible physical body as well as the bio-plasmic body or etheric body that is the energy body that extends beyond the physical body by 4 to 5 inches. The healing here is based upon the two laws namely, the law of self-recovery and the law of *Prana* or life energy. The law of self-recovery is based upon the ability of the body to recover itself without treatment or medicine and the law of *Prana* or life energy is sending or projecting the increased *Prana* to the affected parts and on the entire body. Aroma therapy uses essential oils from plants for healing by inhaling or massaging to enhance physical and psychological well-being. Acupuncture involves penetration of skin with needles to stimulate certain points of the body. This was practiced in China and some Asian countries of the world. It is meant to improve physical health and cure physical and psychological disorders.

In modern times we come across various types of mind-body therapies like cognitive-behavioral Therapy in which patients are taught to tune into the sensations of their body and regulate their breathing to ensure relaxation of muscles to relieve stress by warming their feet and hands, Bio-feedback that trains patients to observe the shifts in their body functions like heart rate, respiration, muscular tension and regulate their activities by using BP electronic monitors so that the patients are able to adjust and modify their mental as well as emotional response that result in lowered blood pressure, lesser anxiety and tension and increased flexibility and so on, and creative art therapies that involve music, art, dance and other creative abilities for reducing depression, anxiety, loneliness, by providing the necessary distraction and create self- awareness and self-esteem in the individual by creating a sense of clarity of vision. There are also many other methods both in the field of medical sciences as well as outside it and in religious and spiritual practices that enhance the overall well-being of a person.

Almost all ancient Indian traditional methods of treatment for the overall health and wellbeing of beings and that are based on the strong foundation of ancient Indian religion of *Sanathana Dharma* or Hinduism and spirituality like *Yoga*, meditation, *Ayurveda*, or the three paths namely the path of devotion, the path of selfless action and the path of knowledge have understood the importance of the integration of body- mind-and spirit for the overall physical, mental and spiritual wellbeing that makes one's life purposeful, worthy, happy and peaceful for oneself and for the others, even from the remote past.

It is heartening to note that the modern youth have started realizing the need for the overall wellbeing that takes into account the inter connection of body, mind and spirit. While some follow one single method there are also others who follow many of these or a combination of some of these. However the goal of all these different methods is the same, namely, Peace and Happiness for man. All the methods whether they are religious and spiritual or otherwise, ancient or modern help man to reach the goal of Peace and Happiness in one's life. If we want to climb up or go upstairs we cannot fly or jump. We need either steps or lift to go up. These methods are like the steps or lift that helps us to reach and achieve the physical, mental and also spiritual well-being".

"Swamiji, is it possible for the modern man to follow the traditional methods in the same way as they were practiced in the past"?

"It is true that all traditional methods for self-development or improvement cannot be practiced exactly as are stated in the scriptures. Since we have to make the necessary modifications depending upon the time in which we are living there is nothing wrong if we make any suitable change in such traditional methods that are appropriate for the modern ways of living. For example in modern times the one who chooses the path of devotion will not be able to follow all the rituals of worship as prescribed in the ancient Indian scriptures as per the procedures laid down there for such practices. Hence necessary changes are to be effected in the methods of worship, so that it is possible for the modern man to follow them. Even in the case of meditation, it is no longer possible for an individual to go to forests, or mountains or caves to practise meditation. What one can do in modern times is to make the surroundings of a room suitable for meditation so that meditation can be carried on in a peaceful atmosphere that is without any hindrance or disturbance."

"Very many techniques that have their roots in the traditional methods are now being propagated by various religious and spiritual masters of today to help man to help himself. The modern man because of increase in population, increase in the number and variety of wants and the resultant scarcity of resources due to over exploitation of resources is liable to become physically, mentally as well as spiritually unhealthy. So he has to find some way or the other to improve himself so that he can lead the best possible life that ensures Peace and Happiness for him. After all it is the goal that matters; but not the means. It is not how we reach the destination but reaching the destination that is what is important. The means may be many but the goal is only one. One can reach a destination by car or bus or train etc. but what is important here is not the type of vehicle that carry us to the destination but the destination itself."

"Swamiji, what are the important ancient Indian traditional methods for holistic health that bring about the best possible life for man?"

"*Ayurveda*, Meditation, *Yoga*, Path of devotion, Path of selfless action, and Path of knowledge are some of the most important ancient paths or techniques that bring about holistic health and thereby the best possible life for man."

"Swamiji, please tell me about Ayurveda that is the ancient system of medical science in India".

"*Ayurveda* is the ancient Indian system of medical science of holistic health that takes in to account the inter relations of body, mind and spirit. It is more than 5000 years old. It is the oldest system of medicine practiced in the world. It is the science of life that is not restricted to merely treating physical illness alone. It has its origin in the *Vedas* of the remote past, particularly the *Rig* and the *Atharva Veda* of the four *Vedas. Ayur* in Sanskrit means life and Veda means knowledge. So *Ayurveda* refers to knowledge about the life of beings as a whole. According to sage *Charaka*, *Ayurveda* is a science that describes *Hitha* or the beneficial and *Ahitha* or non-beneficial aspects of life, the happiness and pain in life, their quality and quantity. It is said that *Ayurveda* had its influences on many traditional systems healing including that of the Tibetan,

Chinese and Greek medicines and therefore it is considered as the mother of all healing systems in the world. This is a treatment or healing technique that stresses the body-mind- spirit interrelationships". Sage *Sushrutha* who was a great exponent of *Ayurveda* defines health as a state of total biological equilibrium where the sensory, mental, emotional, and spiritual elements are harmoniously balanced".

"In *Ayurveda* mental wellbeing is defined as a state of mental, intellectual and spiritual well-being. *Ayurveda* includes meditation, *Yoga*, physical exercises, aromatic oils, diet and medicinal herbs and so on. It focuses itself on how to prevent diseases and how to eliminate their root cause. This system of holistic health lost much of its importance during alien rule. However this holistic healing system has become very popular in recent times".

"The practical aspects of *Ayurveda* known as the *Ashtanga Ayurveda* or the eight limbed *Ayurveda* is divided into eight sections or limbs or branches. These are namely, the *Kaya Chikitsa*, or internal medicine, *Bala Chikitsa* or Pediatrics, *Graha Chikitsa* or Psychological treatment, *Urdhvanga Chikitsa* or treatment of disease above clavicle in head and neck regions, *Shalya Chikitsa* or Surgery, *Damstra Chikitsa* or Toxicology, *Jara Chikitsa* or *Rasayana Chiktsa* or Rejuvenation, *Vajikara Chiktsa* that is treatment relating to fertility".

"*Ayurveda* is based on the supposition that the Universe and beings are made up of five elements namely earth, water, fire, air and space. These elements are represented in the body by three *Doshas*. When any of these three forces accumulates in the body beyond a particular level, then it results in an imbalance in these causing diseases. On the other hand their proper proportion creates good health. Our body and mind are shaped as per the proportion of these three forces. The five elements combine in pairs to constitute these three forces. These are *Vata* that is ether and air, *Piththa*, that is water and fire, and *Kapha* that is water and earth. A person's constitution is determined by the combination of these forces at birth. Hence the treatment has to be as per each person's specific health challenges and needs. So each person gets treatment as per his constitution. Besides medicines this system also stresses on life styles and specific diets, physical activity, external and internal cleanliness".

"The benefits of *Ayurveda* are innumerable. In hastens the healing process in the body. A well regulated diet and lifestyle with the required exercises and enough sleep and rest strengthens the immune system of the body and there by prevents diseases attacking the body. It promotes physical health that leads to mental and spiritual well-being in one by balancing the three forces in the body. It helps in curing diseases like diabetes, heart ailments, cancer, asthma, and tumor and so on. It strengthens all the parts of the body like muscles, bones, heart, liver etc. and maintains blood pressure in the body. It also strengthens the immune system of the body, improves digestion, eliminates toxins in the body and rejuvenates the immune system. At the mental level it has a calming effect on the nerves. It also reduces stress levels, anxiety, tension, etc. resulting in clarity of vision and positive attitude to life resulting in physical, mental and spiritual well-being of a person".

"Swamiji, what is meditation about which so much is said in modern times? How does it help us in achieving our goal?"

"Meditation in Sanskrit is termed as *Dhyana.* It is thinking about one single thought intensely as well as continuously in an effortless manner but not forcefully. It is increased awareness of the mental process. It involves turning inward or concentrating on the inner self. It also means contemplation. It is a process of mental healing- a process to get rid of all mental turmoil and to perceive things as they truly are. It is a tool to discover our inner self. In meditation no force is involved. It does not compel the mind to be calm and quiet but it finds its own way in finding out the silence, calmness and clarity that is there inside our being. Usually meditation is performed with eyes closed or eyes kept open because what is required is one pointed attention. Meditation helps us to know that natural inner silence and make it a part of our life. As we progress we become inspired, get the most intuitive thoughts and come to know the deepest connection between us and the universe and between us the individual soul and the Absolute, the collective, the universal soul. This becomes possible because in meditative state one is in touch with the very core of that one. It is a practice for relaxing and calming the mind as well as the body at the same time. Meditation silences the mind that is chattering continuously inside a being. As we meditate the thoughts disappear or fall off one by one leaving only that single thought that we are contemplating upon. According to *Osho*, meditation means dropping all thoughts from the memory one by one and coming to a state where only the pure consciousness or awareness about oneself remains. It results in a state where the thought of the body, mind and consciousness disappears on its own. When every other thought disappears on its own accord, what remains is one's own real self; the consciousness and that is the ultimate state of meditation. To *Osho* meditation is not merely a practice but an end by itself. It has been an integral part of almost all religions of the world even from the past, even though they are practiced in different ways. Meditation or *Dhyana* is one of the limbs in the *Ashtanga Yoga* of *Patanjali*".

"In the first stage the one who meditates starts contemplating or concentrating on something- certain object or thought. It is in the second stage that concentration becomes meditation. In the third stage he merges with the object of meditation. It is said that in meditation mentally one becomes the object of meditation".

"Once a man went to a sage and asked him about the object of meditation and its effects. The sage then directed the man to contemplate upon God. But the man at once asked the sage, "Why shouldn't I contemplate upon a buffalo instead of God"? The sage immediately told the man to do as he wished as there is nothing wrong in that. The man returned home and he began to meditate upon a buffalo in a very earnest manner. Days and weeks passed. Then one day the sage on his way visited the house of that man and enquired about him. The inmates of the house told the sage that he had gone inside a room for doing meditation and he has been doing it continuously since the time he returned from the *Ashram* of the sage. The sage went near the room and tapped the door and asked the man to come out of the room. After some time the man who was continuously meditating since a few weeks replied, "Oh my dear master, I am unable to come out of this room as my horns are stuck in the door as they are too big and I am not able to free them and come out". It shows that in meditation ultimately a man gets identified with the object of his meditation and he becomes that mentally."

"There are many types and techniques of meditation. Most of these techniques were originated in eastern religions and spirituality. Innumerable varieties of techniques are followed in meditation in modern times by various religious leaders, spiritual masters, in medical science and in holistic health practices. Even in the same religion several sects follow different methods and techniques of meditation. Meditation is practiced by concentrating or contemplating on a single thought that may be any deity, or prayer, or utterance of a *Mantra* that is a combination of core letters or words on a deity or on any spiritual or religious theme, or an idol or even a human being who is one's guru or master or on subtle facts of life. Unlike in worship, in meditation one repeats the single thought upon which he meditates silently. In modern times meditation has become very popular".

"In ancient times meditation was practiced mainly for self-enlightenment the goal of which was spiritual elevation. In modern times it is followed for maintaining and improving physical and also mental health by empowering one with positivity that automatically drives away all the negativity in one. It is the food for the soul and it energizes the mind. It enables the modern man to face all challenges of modern life in a calm and composed, efficient, unperturbed and effective manner as a result of deep inner tranquility".

"Meditation has innumerable benefits. Meditation helps us to know our full potential. A life with fulfillment is possible only when we know our full potential. It enhances the overall wellbeing and creativity. The modern Psycho Therapists have begun to understand, accept and discover various therapeutic benefits of meditation. The great scientists and innovators were able to invent and discover only because they had a continuous, persistent, one pointed attention towards a single thought. The great *Rishis* or sages of India even in the remote past when there were no sophisticated technology as is found today could understand all about the universe, the source of creation and about the created beings of the Universe and they could also reveal through their introspection and meditation how man can become one with the divine. All the material as well as spiritual knowledge they could get as a result of their meditation. When once the mind becomes calm and silent without thoughts then there is clarity in the mind. This clarity of mind enabled the great souls to know all that they wanted to know and practice".

"Meditation generates immense cosmic energy in the meditator. It gives deep rest because the mind is freed from agitation and becomes calm and serene and is at peace. Its flow energizes the entire body, mind and spirit. It helps in cleaning the mind from all unwanted thoughts and channelizes our energy towards one single thought that we want to concentrate or contemplate upon. In meditation our mind gets more focused and this helps us in understanding our own mind more thoroughly. We are able to become aware of our own mind, its powers and its nature in categorizing anything as good or bad. Meditation brings about many physical, physiological, emotional and psychological and spiritual benefits. It results in effective functioning, concentration, self-control, calmness of mind, a relaxed state of mind, enhanced immune system, normalizes weight, brings higher skin resistance, reduces cholesterol levels, reduces the risk of cardio vascular diseases, brings about easier breathing by breathing slowly and deeply, decreases aging process, reduces perspiration, promotes orderliness in brain functioning, reduces the need for medicines, reduces wastage of energy, cures diseases like Asthma, relaxes the nervous system, improves communication, reduces stress, anxiety, depression, headaches, high blood pressure, promotes better observation, results in non-judgmental attitude, increases attention and concentration, sharpens focus and one pointedness, improves memory, blossoms talents and skill, gives relaxation and rejuvenation, improves learning ability, promotes physical, mental and spiritual well-being, provides increased emotional stability, develops intuition, increases productivity, purifies character, develops will power, cures insomnia, enhances the level of self-confidence and reduces the perception of pain, improves relationships, attitudes and responses to any one or any situation of life, and reduces the chronic disorders of the body and mind like fatal and chronic diseases. It brings about a large number of bio chemical changes in the body that alters the heart rate, respiration and so on. It also lowers the stress inducing chemical levels leading to less anxiety and tension. Continuous and prolonged meditation also results in youthful skin and youthful appearance.

Recent studies and research on meditation have shown that meditation increases the intelligence and brain activity and improves awareness and wakefulness and so on. It takes one to a higher state of consciousness spiritually by promoting self-analysis, self-awareness and self-observing attitude. This benefit of meditation has been stressed by many religions and spirituality even from good old days. Meditation promotes peace of mind, happiness and results in wisdom. It enables one to listen to his inner most voice that is his consciousness and makes him a good and valuable human being with all positivity by building up and enhancing the life force. It also turns negativity in to positivity and ultimately brings happiness and peace for the one who meditates and also for the others".

"*Yoga is another technique that is being practiced to a great extent in modern times. So kindly explain to me about that and tell me how it helps man in achieving happiness and peace in life*"?

"The term '*Yoga*' in Sanskrit the ancient language of India means 'Union'. *Yoga* leads to the union of one with his or her real self, or 'God' that is within oneself."

"Yoga is an ancient Indian technique for body-mind harmony and well-being. However in modern times *Yoga* is known by various names depending upon the various organizations particularly spiritual organizations and masters of this technique with slight variations. However the basis for all the various types of *Yoga* that we see and hear today is *Patanjali*'s *Ashtanga Yoga*. *Yoga* as a method promoting body-mind-spiritual well-being with some modern variations is gaining immense popularity even in the western countries today".

"*Patanjali*, the author of ancient Indian classical yoga text, 'The *Yoga Sutra*' defined *Yoga* as the calming down of the fluctuations of mind. The *Yoga Sutra* starts by saying that the purpose of *Yoga* is cessation of *Chitta Vrittis* or the modifications in the mind that arise in the *Chitta.* He says '*Yoga Chitta Vritti Nirodaha*'. *Chitta* is the mind, and *Vritti* refers to thoughts and *Nirodaha* is removal".

"There are eight limbs in the *Ashtanga Yoga* of *Patanjali.* These are, *Yama, Niyama, Asana, Pranayama, Pratyahara, Dharana, Dhyana* and *Samadhi*. Briefly and in a broad sense *Yama* deals with the moral or ethical code of conduct that should be practiced in performing this *Yoga;* *Niyama* relates to self-purification and introspection; *Asana* refers to different postures of the body while performing the different *Yogasana; Pranayama* explains the breathing technique through breath control; *Pratyahara* is withdrawing mind from senses; *Dharana* means concentration on the object of meditation or one pointedness; *Dhyana* is about deep meditation and finally *Samadhi* is a state of union with the object of meditation that leads to the realization of the true identity of oneself."

"The five *yamas or limbs in Patanjali's Ashtanga Yoga* relate to the restraints that one should observe while interacting in the world and that are be followed as social disciplines. These are *Ahimsa* or non-violence, *Satya* or truthfulness, *Asatya* or non- stealing, *Brahmacharya* or celibacy, and *Aparigraha* or non-covetousness. Non-violence is non-injury to any of the beings in creation and is to be practiced in thought, word and deed. Truthfulness is avoiding untruth by expressing and acting with honesty only. Non- stealing is refraining from unauthorized possession of thought, word and deed. Celibacy is avoidance of all sensual and sexual pleasures of life, whether it is mental or physical. Non covetousness is non-accumulation of worldly objects caused by covetousness and attachment.

The *Niyamas* which is the second limb utilizes the energy as a result of following the five *Yamas* that forms the first limb. These help in creating positive environment around us. *Patanjali* mentions five *Niyamas.* These are, *Shucha* that is cleanliness, *Santhosha* or contentment and happiness, *Tapa* or austerity, *Swadhyaya* or self-education and meditation on the divine. In a broad sense, purity deals with both external purity as well as internal, mental purity that are to be obtained by practicing intellectual purity and purity of speech. According to sage *Manu,* water purifies the body, truthfulness purifies the mind and knowledge and austerity purifies the soul. Contentment means not desiring for more than what one gets through his honest labor and what is due to him. It also tells about the quality of equanimity in which one sees all and all situations of life in an equal manner neither getting elated in one or depressed in another, that is, being balanced in happiness or misery, or in favorable or unfavorable situations of life. It also refers to the quality of gratitude and joyfulness, and calmness. Austerity means the power to withstand thirst and hunger, cold and heat, favorable or unfavorable situations, observance of religious rituals and fasts that help in mental as well as physical austerity. Self-education refers to the study of scriptures and understanding them and practicing their contents in one's life. Meditation on the divine is dedicating all intellectual, mental and physical activities to the divine with an attitude of total faith, trust and surrender.

The *Yamas* and *Niyamas* form the guidelines for leading a healthier and happier life. These help in channelizing our energy in a harmonious and integrated manner by complementing our outer life with the understanding of the inner self. They help us to enhance all positive values and thereby make our life happy and peaceful and make our life purposeful and worthy.

The third limb known as the *Asanas* relates to the comfortable and correct postures of the body that facilitate meditation while practicing *Yogasanas*. The *Asanas* are found to have immense therapeutic uses and help in balancing and harmonizing the body structure as the *Asanas* are designed to release tension, improve flexibility, and maximize the flow of vital energy. It is told that these postures perform five important functions namely conative that means the voluntary exercise of the organs of action, cognitive when the *Asanas* or postures create a flow of positive energy and make concentration turn inward so that the mind is in a position to perceive its positive effects, mental that is the mental awareness due to conative and cognitive actions that flow in our body leading to a mental state of pure and unlimited joy, and the intellectual and spiritual functions because of the influence of the physical postures on the various interrelated *Nadis* or channels of mind-body complex. The performance of *Yogasanas* result in absolute intellectual absorption of the mind on a single task namely *Dharana* that leads to the fusion of the individual spirit with divinity that can be termed as *Dyana*. There are various *Asanas* and these are, standing *Asanas*, forward bending *Asanas*, inverted *Asanas*, abdominal *Asanas*, twisting *Asanas*, back bending *Asanas* and so on.

The fourth limb of *Astanga Yoga* is *Pranayama*. It is about controlling the *Prana* or the life force through breath control. It is understood that breath is intimately connected to our emotional state of being. It is also found that breath has the power to access our subconscious and all the behavioral patterns in it. It can transform and release these and also access unconscious material within us. There are various types of *Pranayama* that are practiced.

The fifth limb of *Yoga* is *Pratryahara* that deals with the right management of the senses and going beyond the senses for the proper understanding of one's real self.

Dharana that forms the sixth limb gives various ways to direct and channelize our attention and mind inward.

Dhyana that is the seventh limb is a state of meditation, a state of awareness where the mind gets one pointed attention without any distractions and disturbances.

Samadhi that is the final limb of *Patanjali*'s *Ashtanga Yoga* is the total absorption state of a being. At this stage the *Yogi* becomes one with the truth and he merges with the object of his concentration. Here the perceiver, the perceived both become one and the same- as there is merger of these two".

"A regular practice of *Yoga* has immense effects on the physical and mental health. It enhances our life energies and the creative abilities in us. It also helps in reducing the cholesterol levels of the body, reduces over weight, normalizes the blood pressure and improves the performance of the heart leading to greater vitality and decreased stress. It also helps in clearing the blockages in the mind, maintains mental balance and calmness. These also make the mind strong and enable the physical body to withstand pain or misery in a calm and composed manner. The practice of *Yoga* also results in inner peace, and awareness of our essential true nature. It is found to be the best effective method for stress reduction by offering numerous tools to shift the balance of the autonomic nervous system to the Para sympathetic side. It also calms the mind and lowers the levels of stress hormones like Cortisol. It is also found to give relief to many stress related conditions such as insomnia, irritable bowel syndrome characterized by cramping, abdominal pain, bloating, constipation, diarrhea, heart diseases, hypertension, and diabetes and so on. It is also found to be effective in treating asthma, arthritis, heart problems and so on. The practice of Yoga also provides increased strength and flexibility, better balance and coordination, better lung function and weight loss. Its psychological effects include a relaxed state of mind, greater balance of mind leading to equanimity, better concentration and happy mood. *Pranayama* results in inner peace and tranquility by manipulating the inner energy through the full utilization of the lung capacity for breathing. It helps in releasing tension and develops a relaxed state of mind. It increases the amount of oxygen to the brain resulting in improved mental clarity and alertness and physical well-being. It also enhances the concentration levels. It is also said to balance the functions of the neuro-endocrine system of the body that is the system of glands that secret different types of hormones directly in to the blood stream that play a vital part in constituting the temperament or nature of a person. However *Yoga* is to be practiced only with the help of a trained master of *Yoga* as any wrong method of breathing or *Pranayama* and the *Yogasanas* or the *yoga* postures will lead to harmful results".

"What are the Indian traditional religious that are also spiritual paths for self-development or for self-improvement to reach the goal of Peace and Happiness Swamiji"?

"The path of devotion, the path of selfless service and the path of knowledge are the three important traditional paths advocated by the ancient Indian spirituality and religion for improving oneself or for elevating one's mind that result in physical, mental or psychological and spiritual well-being".

"The path of devotion everyone knows to a certain extent. But I would like to know from you Swamiji, the meaning of real devotion and how it helps us in achieving our goal of life?"

"The path of devotion has been stressed by all the religions of the world. It is called *Bhakthi Marga* in Sanskrit language. All religions teach and stress upon the ethical and positive values for enhancing one's physical and mental health and spirituality. The path of devotion is nothing but a way of life. A real devotee always remembers God without any effort because he has some kind of very intimate relationship with him that makes him love God, think about his chosen deity in an automatic manner continuously without any effort. It is not merely remembering god because remembering anything has a meaning only when we forget anything even for a very brief time period. But the real devotee is one who cannot forget the memory of God even for a short time. When that is so, where is the question of bringing back the memory of God or remembering God comes? A mother of a new born baby, whatever may be the work she is engaged in, constantly remembers the child and his needs. Similarly the devotee who though is in the midst of worldly life never is able to forget God. He will have the thought of God always in his mind. For him it is almost like breathing. He cannot lead his life without the presence of God in his mind. The essential character and basis of devotion is love and service to God with total faith, trust and surrender of the body, mind and spirit to the will of God or the Almighty.

A truly religious person through his humility, his faith and devotion on the supreme power is able to hear and understand his inner voice and lead his life without becoming a prey to the evil tendencies which we categorize as negative. He also makes himself as pure as possible by remembering God, his ideal always and following the teachings of the enlightened souls.

Prayer that is an important aspect of the path of devotion is rooted in the belief that there is that Supreme, Absolute power that created this world, and governs everything in this universe. For a real devotee God is a reality while for the non-believers it is mere imagination. This path involves going to temples, *Satsangh* or being in good company, performing rituals and worship, unselfish service to the lord, study of scriptures, singing *Bhajans*, listening to devotional music and so on as a regular practice so that all these or at least a few of these become a part of one's life like eating, sleeping talking and so on. All these are meant to keep the body, mind and the spirit healthy and to prevent mind from thinking self-destructive thoughts that lead to negativity.

In this path of devotion to God it is the heart or emotion that dominates and culminates in devotion. Here the mind and its reasoning disappear to a great extent. A true devotee will not be able to reason out why he loves and trusts God. A true devotee is a sincere and true lover of God, the divine. His love is not seeking anything from God or the divine. The emotion that is found in the beginning stages becomes total devotion, leading to trust and then surrender and in the final stage of his devotion the devotee dissolves into his object of devotion. So the devotee also becomes as pure as his object of worship and the purity in him is revealed through his virtues that refer to all moral and ethical codes of conduct.

All religions teach what is best for one and all. A truly religious person is one who seeks welfare for one and all in the universe, whatever may be the religion that he follows. He sees the Almighty everywhere and anywhere. He is the one who understands the real meaning of worship, rituals and prayers.

In the beginning stages a devotee may pray to God for the fulfillment of his wishes and he may be performing all the rituals, methods of worship and may pray to his chosen deity for this purpose. He may also do all these in a mechanical manner because of his conditioning or belief system from childhood or he also may have a feeling that if he does not pray to God and perform the necessary acts of worship then God may get angry and he will punish him and so on. Such thoughts disappear from him when he becomes a true devotee of his chosen deity. Instead of fear there will be unconditional total unselfish love, trust, and surrender. At this stage he does not pray for the fulfillment of his wishes. He prays to God to make him purer and purer so that he can be an embodiment of all virtues of life. Prayer helps him to become humble, become less egoistic and reduce all negative tendencies and fills his mind with positivity. His ego gets dissolved in the object, or idol or deity of his worship. Thus the path of devotion becomes a suitable path for self- improvement to all alike. Unlike in the case of worldly life, if a person trusts God then he is sure to be rewarded. The trust that one reposes on another may not be lasting as there is every possibility that the trust is misused by the person who is trusted. But when you trust and surrender yourself completely to the existence itself, to the divine power, to God then there cannot be any cheating but total destruction of your ignorance. Does that mean that when we pray to Him, God will grant us all that we want? Ask a few. But God is not for granting wishes. With total trust if one can adhere to all that any religion teaches then he will come to know that the fulfillment of material desires is not that, that matters at all. No doubt one needs to have material wellbeing as well. But a truly religious person will never crave for more and more of the material pleasures and possessions as he realizes that too much of material desires will only ruin a person with all negative qualities. He will also be in a position to become calm and relaxed as he lives without much tension and anxiety as he knows that whatever is due to him he is sure to get and he takes the support or help of the divine in elevating his mind so that he can face any good or bad situations of life with equanimity. He also gets a feeling that he is not alone but God the divine is there to guide him and support him in every situation provided he follows the path of righteous living that upholds all positive qualities or what we call as virtues.

A real devotee is one who prays for one and all, for the welfare of all. In such an act he not only generates but also sends immense positive energy to others around him and he fills the atmosphere with positive energy. So he is in a position to build up a lot of positive energy not only for himself but for the others as well. A pseudo devotee on the other hand prays for his well- being only and for the fulfillment of his desires even at the expense of others. At times he may even pray for the downfall of others so that he can come up in life. Such people spread out negative energy everywhere and ultimately that negative energy comes back to them causing their own downfall. Prayer is meant not for causing harm to anyone but only for the wellbeing of one and all on earth".

"All negative emotions crop up in the mind because of ego that leads to desire, attachment and expectations. Ego is the real barrier that puts hurdles in improving oneself. It is because of ego that all negative qualities crop up in the mind of man. Once the ego dissolves then all that we call good or positive will find a place in the heart and mind. All religions teach man to be humble. All religions speak of God who is omnipresent, omniscient and omnipotent and who is all powerful and who is the creator of everything that we see in this Universe. The belief in that supreme power makes a truly religious person but not a pseudo devotee to be humble. When a person is humble his ego cannot raise its head. Once the ego is low then undue desires, expectations, attachments etc. will disappear from one's mind and there will be no room for negativity in man. All religions also teach man to be morally good and follow the righteous path that contains all virtues for reaping all that are good ultimately".

"In this method the devotee may have devotion to God in some form or other or to an *Avatar* or God in human form or to some spiritually elevated person who is master and guide and who is considered as God by the devotee.

In Hinduism God the almighty is represented by an idol. Here the size of the idol or the thing with which the idol is made up of is not at all important for the devotee. The idol might have been made up of mud, clay, wood or metal or with any other material. But the devotee is not bothered about this. This is because the devotee sees God or his deity in that idol. To him the idol that he worships represents the all-pervading supreme power, the Almighty. Whether he performs *Abhishekam* that is the sacred bath for the idol, whether he decorates the idol with flowers and ornaments, whether he offers *Naivedyam*, the food offerings to the idol, whether he performs worship to the idol and chants prayer – all these he does with the belief and faith that the idol represents the Almighty. The real devotee knows fully well that God is omnipotent, omnipresent and omniscient. Since it is impossible to visualize and concentrate on that energy that has no form or name, the humans give some form or name to that supreme power. This is the basis of idol worship in Hinduism. Worshipping the

Absolute energy with some form enables the devotee to concentrate on the all-pervading energy through the idol. It also facilitates the devotee to meditate upon his chosen deity very easily and to offer his prayers and perform various rituals associated with prayer and worship.

Actually during Vedic period there was no idol worship. But as time passed sanctity and purity in humans decreased so also their spiritual potential and powers. The sages or the *Rishis* then realized that under the changed scenario it is difficult for all to concentrate on the formless abstract energy because it was difficult for the human mind to understand and remember anything that has no form and name. So the *Rishis*, the sages created Gods and Goddesses with some form or other that mostly depicted their qualities represented by the idols of worship.

However all the rituals of worship or chanting of prayers for the unborn child from the time when the child is in its mother's womb and that continues even after one's death in the form of prayers and rituals for the departed souls are meant only to build up and radiate positive energy. So once we are able to generate positive energy through positive thoughts, words and deeds then we are doing a great service not only to humanity as a whole but to all beings of the universe and this is the fundamental basis of Hinduism the ancient religion of India. Even the *Shanthi Mantras* that are found in the *Upanishads* are meant for the well-being of the entire universe that is considered as the *Vasudeva Kutumbhakam* or the single global family. Viewing the entire universe as a single family is unique to Hinduism".

"Some people ask about the contradiction that they find in divine blessings on account of devotion on the one hand and the law of *Karmic* effect on the other. They say does the path of *Bhakthi* ensure that the all-powerful God will shower His blessings on his devotee and grant him all that he wishes for in his life? Can one who is a devotee, who has immense faith in God will be pardoned by his deity for all the bad or harm that he has committed to the others in thought, words and deeds and undo their bad effects on the devotee? If God does not or cannot do this then how can we call him all powerful and the one who protects His devotees? On the other hand suppose God protects His devotee from all the ill effects of his bad *Karmas* or past deeds then how can the law of *Karma* that says what we sow we reap or what we give we get hold good? This is no doubt a good question that needs to be answered for removing the confusion caused by the ignorance of the one who is asking such a question. First of all God is that all pervading energy that does not take sides. He or it is meant not for granting blessings. For example a doctor who has a nursing home or hospital of his own may pray for more and more patients to visit his hospital so that he can get back all that he has invested on that and also more than that. On the other hand no one will ever want to become sick as each will pray only for a disease free life. When God hears both their prayers whose side will He take? Such notions that God is meant for granting blessings is childish. It may be useful to make children good because children cannot understand the fundamental lofty truths. But an adult should know that energy is only an impartial witness to everything. It does not punish one for one's wrong doing or bless another for his righteousness. The person on account of his *Karmas*, in accordance with the law of *Karma* reaps the benefits of his past *karmas* that comes to him in the course of time, either in the form of divine blessings or in the form of miseries and unhappiness on account of his past wrong or negative thoughts, words or deeds. Just as some seeds sprout quickly while others take more time to become seedlings similarly the effects of some *Karmas* are quick whereas that of the others get delayed as their effects are experienced only after a long period of time. But one will necessarily enjoy the benefits of his good *Karmas* and will have to reap the bad effects of negative or evil *Karmas*. This is inevitable. That is why we find some people who are really good suffering in this world while people who are bad are successful and enjoy their life. Some children are born lame or blind etc. Why? The only explanation is the inevitable operation of the law of *Karma* in their life.

The *Karma* theory however relates to our past *Karmas* only. But as far as the present *Karmas* are there, we know as human beings we are endowed with intelligence that has discriminating ability. Man is the only being in creation that has got the freedom and choice to do either good or positive or bad or negative. If we choose the righteous path we practise and do all that are good or positive on account of our virtues and if we choose to be bad or negative then we fill ourselves with all types of negativity that will ruin us. But it is up to one to choose to be positive and good rejecting all that are bad or negative. If a person is very bad and full of negativity and if he is still blessed with all that he wants in life and on account of that if he is happy then it must be because he has not exhausted the effects of his past positivity. Contrary to this if one is very good and still if he is unhappy now it is because he has not exhausted the effects of his past negative karmas yet. Only when the effect of his past positivity fructifies he will be able to reap all its benefits. The devotee is one who seeks God's help and guidance in everything with a humble heart and he knows for certain that God will help only those who help themselves by doing all that are possible to fill him with positivity. So it is the effect of our past *Karmas* that we are reaping in the present birth. Similarly our future life also depends upon our present tendencies, feelings and emotions that become our words and actions in the present. The great Indian sages of the past therefore compared all our thoughts, words and actions that we have thought, spoken or put in to action in our past with the released arrow that will hit the target once it is released from the bow. Even the bowman who has released the arrow from his bow has no control over the arrow because the released arrow cannot be made to change its course. But as far as our present state is concerned it is like the arrow that is yet to be released from the bow. The bowman has got the freedom to release the arrow in whichever direction he wants. So also is the case with our present tendencies that will result in either bad or good, happiness and peace or unhappiness and lack of peace. It all depends on whether we release the positive vibrations or the negative ones and one thing that is certain is that all positive will come back to us even in greater measure so also our negative emotions will result in the return of negativity either in the same or in greater proportions.

Our prayers cleanse our mind and a pure mind cannot but be all positive that generates and projects positivity that will result in a happy and peaceful life. A real devotee is able to imbibe all that are positive in the world and in course of time he becomes an embodiment of all that are virtuous and righteous and he cannot but think, speak and do all that are good that yield good effects later. Such a one will also be in a position to empower himself with more and more of positive energy without much effort. This is the effects of prayer and the devotee knows this fully well. A true devotee who never expects God to fulfill his desires has a firm conviction that while all worldly attachments and bondage ultimately lead to unhappiness and misery though they give enjoyment and pleasure temporarily, his attachment and bondage to God yield nothing but happiness and peace. While all worldly relationships end in disempowering one ultimately due to expectation and attachments and so on, true devotion results in empowering and enriching oneself to face all situations of life in an easy and proper manner. While worldly bondage enslaves us, the bondage that one has with the Almighty gives him real freedom from all sorrows and miseries of life".

"What do we mean by the path of selfless action? How does this virtue bring about Peace and Happiness for man?"

"The path of action is called *Karma Marga* in Sanskrit. This is the path of selfless service to others in thought, word and deed. The path of selfless service or action requires that one performs positive actions based on his positive thoughts for the welfare of others without least expectation of any return, with no feeling of doership or without any concern for the welfare of one's own self.

One who is inclined to do selfless service may do it for the welfare of others no doubt, but in a very subtle manner, it is possible, that he may expect some appreciation or popularity or he may do selfless service with the thought that by such deeds and words he is acquiring lot of merits that will come to his rescue when he himself becomes helpless. He may feel if I perform selflessly now may be some day somebody else will do the same thing for me and help me in times of need. It is like saving money for our financial security in future so that financial crisis in future can be overcome with the help of one's past savings. But as and when one gets a taste of selfless service, he will start forgetting himself and the one single goal for such a person will be to sacrifice even his life for the sake of others. What offering can be more noble and divine than this? His actions will also be without the least expectation of reward or appreciation of any kind. He is also never bothered whether his selfless service is being praised or criticized by the others. For such a person the welfare of the others is the only agenda in his life.

While doing such a service one should never become proud of himself with the thought and feeling that he has done something great and as such he is undoubtedly a great person and no others could have done it like him. Such actions should come from him automatically and naturally like the flow of river, without any conscious effort on his part. Only a person who overflows with virtues or positive qualities like Love, sacrifice, kindness, empathy, compassion, and so on can do such selfless service. When a person tries to save another person who is trapped in the flames, he does not think about the risk involved to his own life in such an act because to him saving the other person is the only important thing. Often such acts are done in a spontaneous manner when positive emotions dominate in one. If one can make such feeling his very nature then he becomes divine. Such people who are full of divinity are however rare. Even if all cannot reach that level at least every one can try to be as selfless as possible in their thoughts, words, and actions".

"The *Karma* path or the path of selfless service is based upon the belief that each of our *Karma* creates an invisible account by creating some energy that is either positive or negative that is the result of positive thought, word or deed, or negative word or deed. The thoughts in whichever form it is, gets stored up and gets recorded in our subconscious mind. More and more positive thoughts that come out as words and deeds generate or deposit more and more positive energy in our account and will result in more and more happiness to one. On the other hand more and more negativity in the form of negative thoughts, words and actions will result in more and more negative energy in our account resulting in more and more unhappiness and misery to us sooner or later".

"Sometimes when we do our duties as per our role in life as parent, offspring etc. we claim that we are following the path of

Karma or selfless action. But when we look at such actions intensely we will come to know that there is an element of selfish love that has some expectation or other that makes us do such service. Even parents have some expectations from their grown up children. May be when the children are quite young the parents do everything for them without the least expectation of anything in return. But when they grow up the parents expect at least recognition for their selfless service towards their children. But then we should know that it is the duty of the parents to be unselfish and work selflessly for their children. Like teachers, doctors, lawyers, farmers etc. they are also doing their duty only. That means one who does selfless service as per his role in life or as per his profession is only doing his duty sincerely. It is not the path of *Karma.* One can be said to be following the path of selfless service or the path of *Karma* only when he serves the others without selfish motive and without any expectation. He must also be one for whom the welfare of the others is the primary concern even by ignoring or setting aside his own welfare and he serves one and all even when he is not bound to serve them that is even though it is not his duty, that is, as per his role or profession.

The one who is inclined to follow this path possesses positive values or virtues like unselfish love, kindness, empathy, compassion etc. and is ready to sacrifice and forego his well-being for the benefit of others and is also prepared to undergo any amount of hardship for the sake of others. Such acts make one pure at heart without any cleansing process and generate positive energy in him and it makes his life immensely happy and peaceful."

"*Tell me also about the path of knowledge, Swamiji, and also how it helps one in making one's life worthy, purposeful, happy and peaceful*"?

"In the path of knowledge it is the head that is dominating. In this path one tries to acquire the relevant knowledge from various sources like scriptures, spiritual masters, and *Sat sang* and so on to uplift himself. It is not worldly knowledge or the knowledge that belongs to the material world. It is a spiritual quest to know about oneself. After acquiring the relevant knowledge or *Gnana* one who follows this path will ponder over the knowledge that is in the form of information. In the third stage he will contemplate upon his self through self-enquiry to understand the truth. In such a process he will also come to know what are thoughts, How do they appear in one's mind? What is mind? How can vices be eliminated? What are virtues? How do they help man in achieving everlasting peace and happiness? Is he the body or mind or the inner energy and so on and so forth. The self-enquiry ultimately enables him to experience the truth and he attains *Vijnana* or wisdom. That one who gains the necessary wisdom becomes totally pure and he goes beyond all dualities of life. The one who has thus become spiritually wise will have happiness, peace, equanimity, tolerance, kindness, love, compassion, humility, truthfulness, honesty, integrity, openness of heart and so on. In short such a person will become an embodiment and personification of all virtues and he who is always blissful will also make the others happy and at peace".

"A sincere, whole hearted, honest and continuous practise of any single of the above mentioned methods or a combination of all these methods will result in happiness and peace in the world as a whole making every one's life in this world the Best possible. However a devotee who expects God to fulfill all his desires of life cannot transform his mind. He should instead understand that God the supreme is the source of all positivity and purity and as such he should seek His help and grace for obtaining the necessary wisdom to imbibe all positive virtues of life and make continuous efforts to practice all the virtues so that the virtues will become his very nature. Similarly one who does some service to others in a selfish manner anticipating some reward or return cannot become a true follower of self-less action. He must know that the soul in each one of us is the same as that Absolute soul whom we call as God and any service done in a selfless manner to anyone is service to himself and God. Then only he will be able to become positive in his thought, word and deed and attain the necessary wisdom to make his life the Best possible. So also a man who follows the path of knowledge should know that mere knowledge will not help him in any way. Once he comes to know through knowledge that he is not the body or mind but the inner energy that is the same in all then he will not see anybody as different from him and he will make his life the Best possible by thinking, speaking and doing positively. So whichever of the three paths one chooses he should practise it with full knowledge of the path and its ultimate objective. For such a one the possibility of the 'Best Possible Life' that yields happiness and peace is not a far off but a destination that he can reach in no time".

Suddenly I woke up hearing my husband's voice. "Get up, the train is nearing *Palakkad* junction".

After I woke up and came to my senses I realized that the entire conversation between me and the *Swamiji*- the questions I put to him and his replies were all only my dream. However I mentally thanked the *Swamiji* for all his contribution to my new work, all the knowledge that he imparted to me through my dream as it gave me enough and more material for my forthcoming book.

"Where is that *Sanyasi* with whom you were talking"? I asked my husband.

"Really it was a very useful talk. I wish he could have continued his journey at least until we got down so that I could have listened to him the whole night. But unfortunately he got down at *Salem* itself. My mind was so full of all that he told that I never wanted to sleep as I was remembering and enjoying all that he said about the places and the temples he visited and about those spiritual masters he had the opportunity to meet in the Himalayan regions and their discourses and his experiences. My mind was so full of all that he told that it was nearly half past five by the time I got some sleep" replied my husband.

The train was speeding and finally it entered the 'Gods own country'-*Kerala*. It was passing through the *Valayar* forest and it was a thrilling and wonderful sight. The train was running late. It was already 7.30 in the morning. Even after sunrise there was total darkness throughout the forest as it was full of tall trees that stood very close to each other. Only the humming of the bees and the strange sound of the wind that the train was cutting through one could hear. It was rainy season and there were thick clouds on the sky giving us a signal that any moment it is going to rain heavily. Within no time it began to drizzle. Both my mind and body became so fresh that I felt a great sense of enjoyment and happiness inside me and even at this age I felt like dancing like a small girl in the showers.

"I am very happy now. The *Swamiji* gave me all material for my new book" I told my husband.

"No chance. What are you saying? When did he speak to you at all? Even before the train reached *Jolarpet* junction you were fast asleep. Then how could you ever talk to him in the first place?"

Then I told my husband all about my dream and my intention to start writing the book that very day lest I may forget that dream of mine. My husband jokingly remarked "That means I can escape myself from listening to your usual discourses for some time- until you complete your new book". Then looking at my expression he continued, "What I mean is"....

Just then the mobile phone rang and it was our son on the other side. "Have you reached *Palakkad*? How was the journey? Did you sleep well? Are you both alright? Take good rest. Do not strain much". Our son went on with his nonstop questions.

"The train is late by an hour. Only just now we got down from the train. Both of us are quite fine. We had a wonderful journey and both of us enjoyed it well. Don't worry about us. Take care .We will take care of ourselves. By the way, you know *Amma* could gather all the necessary material for her new book. She is so happy", said my husband.

"How?" He eagerly asked.

I took the phone from my husband and said "Hallo, *Ponnumon* (This is how I call him) I shall explain to you all about it later. Take care. You can be rest assured that as per your wish the next book of your *Amma* is going to be a mixture of information and her imagination although I cannot say how it will turn out to be. I hope you are happy now".

"Yes of course. Anyway, don't bother about its outcome. All right?" he replied.

Again my husband continued "What I meant was—, you will find only a little time to spare for me once you start writing your new book because you will be totally engrossed in that".

"Yes, yes, don't I know you? Can't we and don't we understand each other thoroughly even after so many years of our life together? I can read your thoughts just as you can read mine" I said. At this remark my husband laughed heartily and I joined him in his hearty laughter.

My husband's nephew, who had come to receive us at the station was coming towards us. He greeted us and enquired whether we had a comfortable journey. In turn I and my husband enquired about his welfare and that of all the others at home. He then took our luggage and the three of us walked out of the station.

That very evening after my twilight prayers I started writing this book lest I may forget any single bit of my dream that I stored up in my memory on that night of my journey and this book is the outcome of that dream and my late twilight musings.